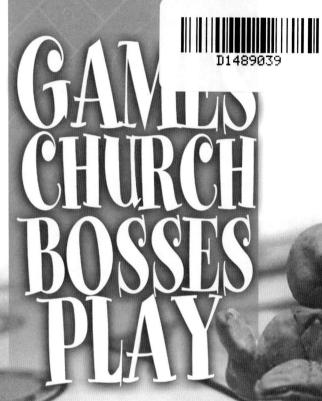

GAMES CHURCH BOSSES PLAY

Carl R. Hobbs

Pathway PRESS

D1489039

Book Editor: Wanda Griffith
Editorial Assistant: Tammy Hatfield
Copy Editors: Cresta Shawver
Oreeda Burnette
Inside Layout: Mark Shuler

Library of Congress Catalog Card Number: 00-105-729
ISBN: 0-87148-945-7
Copyright © 2000 by Pathway Press
Cleveland, Tennessee 37311
All Rights Reserved
Printed in the United States of America

Dedication

This book is dedicated to the pastors and their families who are out there faithfully serving in ministry and contending with the "accuser of the brethren."

Table of Contents

Acknowledgments

Special thanks go to . . .

- *Sharon*, my faithful companion of 40 years, who spent long hours typing and retyping this manuscript. She bears in her body the battle scars from our time in pastoral ministry.

- *Lance Colkmire*, coworker and children's pastor extraordinaire, who edited the manuscript before it was revised and forwarded to the publisher.

- Thanks also to several pastors who shared their stories with me privately or at public gatherings. They shall remain anonymous.

- A word of appreciation should also be given to Book Editor *Wanda Griffith*, and the copy editors who made it possible for this book to meet publishing and marketing deadlines.

Introduction

As a teenager, I occasionally had the privilege of traveling to various state and national church conventions with a carload of pastors. The stories they told were fascinating. Frequently these stories gravitated toward two major themes—local church finances and local church bosses.

My young mind often thought that surely these tales of woe were grossly exaggerated and blown out of proportion. Then I grew up and pastored a church and discovered that "the half has not been told"—especially regarding stories of local church bosses.

Now as the sun is beginning to set on my ministerial career, it seems like the right time to express publicly what pastors and their families have been discussing privately for generations. Little has been written regarding local church bosses up to the present time.

I would like to suggest two reasons that the literature is so scarce in the area of the abuse of pastors and their families by local church bosses. First, if a pastor is still in active ministry, there is some risk of reprisal. Second, if the pastor is retired and, therefore, out of the reach of his former antagonists, he probably does not wish to recall the painful encounters, much less write about them.

The most frequent question asked by friends and colleagues as this manuscript was being written was, "Which church bosses are you talking about, the hierarchy of the church or local church bosses?" The response was quick and to the point—local church bosses. The question, however, does point out the need for a working definition of a "local church boss." In addition to some of the more colorful descriptions found in the text, the following will serve as our working definition:

> A local church boss is a person in the local congregation who, for selfish reasons, attempts to use his or her power or influence as leverage to dictate church policy decisions or to gain a measure of control over the pastor and his vision for the congregation.

It should be noted that there is a vast difference between a local church boss and a local church leader. Bosses hinder progress and attempt to bind the hands of the pastor, staff and governing body of the church. Local church leaders, on the other hand, promote progress and support the pastor and his staff in ministry.

Perhaps John C. Maxwell said it best in an excerpt from his book *Developing the Leader Within You*:

> The boss drives his men; the leader coaches them.
> The boss depends upon authority; the leader on good will.
> The boss inspires fear; the leader inspires enthusiasm.
> The boss says "I"; the leader, "We."
> The boss fixes the blame for the breakdown; the leader fixes the breakdown.
> The boss knows how it is done; the leader shows how.
> The boss says "Go"; the leader says "Let's go!"[1]

This book is written primarily for pastors to let them know they are not alone in their suffering. There is life and joy on the other side of these dark encounters with local church bosses. Should this book fall into the hands of concerned laity, may it increase their awareness about the abuse of pastors and their families by local church bosses.

Perchance should a local church boss read this book, it is hoped it will bring about repentance and spiritual renewal.

Disclaimer

The anecdotal stories in this book regarding encounters between pastors and local church bosses are all based on true accounts. Names have been omitted to protect the innocent and not give the guilty cause for complaint. I believe these events are so common among pastors across all denominational lines that any attempt to relate them to real people—living or dead—would be virtually impossible.

By Ned

1

Breaking Glass and the Railroad Crossing

The sound coming from the bathroom in the church parsonage were a mixture of low moans and breaking glass. The pastor was sitting in the den. His first thought was that his wife had dropped a hair dryer into a sink full of water and was being electrocuted.

Jumping up, he ran toward the bathroom. Glass objects were flying out of the bathroom door and breaking against the hallway wall. The low moan he had heard from the den now became words of despair repeated over and over. His wife had mentally snapped. She was throwing and breaking anything she could get her hands on and repeating, "It's not supposed to be like this. It's not supposed to be like this."

Wrapping his arms around her and pinning her arms to her sides, he held her close for a long time, while speaking soothing words in her ear. She had struck the ceramic sink with such force, she had knocked a hole in it about the size of a half dollar. He knew his wife was very close to a complete mental breakdown.

How had they come to this tragic state of affairs? They were good people, trying to do the will of the Lord by shepherding one of His flocks. Neither of them had been raised in a parsonage, but from the time they met as teenagers and fell in love, they knew God had special work for them to do.

They married young and both worked to put him through school—first Bible college and eventually a doctor of education degree from a major state university. Their future seemed secure. He accepted a position as a public school teacher and eventually became an elementary school principal. Life was good. They bought a house and increased their family. They already had a son and now added a little girl. Other than some initial health problems with the children, their family was complete and they were content—almost. There was a nagging restlessness in their hearts to be involved in full-time ministry.

Their opportunity came when a former Bible college professor phoned and invited them to come to the West Coast and work with him at a small private sectarian college where he had recently been appointed president. He was thrilled, but his wife was traumatized by the thought of selling their home, uprooting their family and moving all the way across the country. Eventually, he won the debate, and they loaded the U-Haul and headed west. After a period of adjustment, they loved their work and their new home. They both worked at the college: she in the business office and he as a professor and administrator. Life was good. Now they could combine ministry and education. It was the perfect situation.

The West Coast was wonderful. It had everything—mountains, ocean, deserts, orchards and big cities rich with culture. They could have stayed forever; but after 11 years, the college fell on hard times financially and the church transferred them back east. Since there were no immediate openings at the denomination's main campus, church officials asked them if they would consider pastoring. They reluctantly agreed, reminding the church officials that their background was in education and not pastoral work, even though they had helped to train over 1,000 young men and women for ministry.

Maybe they were tired of being armchair quarterbacks in ministry. Maybe it was a desire to remain in full-time ministry. Maybe it was because their options were limited. For all the above and several other reasons, they said, "Yes, we will pastor a church." Financially, the package of salary and benefits was roughly equivalent to their package at the college. Again they loaded the U-Haul and headed off to their new assignment.

At the college, he might have the opportunity to address the student body in chapel once or twice a year. Now he would be responsible for two sermons on Sunday and a Bible study midweek. This, plus some counseling and home and hospital visitation, would be their main challenges . . . or so they thought. They had no idea what awaited them.

It did not take long for them to meet their major challenge—the notorious blue-bellied, swallow-tailed church boss, or *terroronicus pastoras* (the terror of pastors).[1] He did not look too imposing the first time they saw him. He showed up with some of his cronies to help them unload the U-Haul. He was small in stature and a senior citizen. How tough could he be? The newly appointed pastor towered over him and was perhaps 30 years his junior. He could take him on his worst day with one hand tied behind his back—or so he thought. The pastor grossly underestimated this man. His reputation was well-known, attested to by every former pastor by the tearstains found in the parsonage. The pastor was determined that this man would not get the best of him.

The church boss wasted no time in establishing the rules of the game. Even while they were unloading the furniture, he informed the pastor which staff members were worth keeping and which ones should be fired immediately. When the pastor told him that as senior pastor, he planned to take the first three to six months to evaluate staff, the layman seemed a bit startled that his advice had not been taken at face value. The pastor did not know it then, but he had just fought round one of an epic battle that would go on for almost three years. This game might be called "shadow boxing," but it soon turned into a bare-knuckled fight.

Round one had been a warm-up and would have been judged more or less a draw. The lessons I learned about conflict resolution and strategies in dealing with church bosses form the basis for this book. Others have suffered more and could have told their stories more eloquently; but for some reason the Holy Spirit has laid this burden on my heart and prompted me to share this story.

Not long after I found my wife in the bathroom breaking glass, I attended a meeting where a former pastor of my congregation was one of the speakers. I had always wanted to meet him because he was living testimony that there was life beyond the pastorate of that particular congregation, so I listened intently as the guest speaker spoke. What he said was startling.

The speaker recounted a time, in the not-too-distant past, when he was pastoring a particular church. On the way home late one evening, he approached a railroad crossing where a train was coming. As he slowly approached the tracks, a siren voice whispered, "Don't stop." It was so real that it startled him. For a moment he considered obeying the voice. He thought, *My church and family would think it was an accident. I'd receive a Christian burial, and no one would know I committed suicide.* He hesitated just long enough for the train to pass by without incident; but the thought of what he had just considered rattled his foundation.

What caused an experienced pastor to consider suicide? His presentation gave insight. He had been practicing "shuttle diplomacy" at his church, running back and forth between the warring factions. In trying to please everyone, he was pleasing no one. He was mentally, physically and spiritually exhausted. Suicide seemed like a reasonable option.

I sat there with tears streaming down my face. I wondered how many other pastors were driven to this point of despair. How many not only had considered suicide but actually carried through with their plans?

I remembered the circus performer who balances plates on flexible poles. One at a time he starts them spinning, and just as the first one loses momentum, he runs back and gives it new life. Running from pole to pole, and plate to plate, each time starting a new plate spinning, the circus performer eventually has several plates in the air. Logic says that even the best performer has his limitations. There will come a time when just one more spinning plate will cause all the plates to come crashing down.

So it is with pastors who practice "shuttle diplomacy" among warring factions in their congregations. There will come a time when just one more spinning plate will cause their whole ministry to come crashing down. How many hunting accidents or single-car wrecks were intentional? We will never know. The sad thing is that ministers are driven to this point of self-destruction but not by outside persecution or pressures. The enemy is within the church walls, masquerading as a friend of the church who thinks he is doing God a service by launching relentless attacks on the minister and his family. Jesus said there would be such people (see John 16:1-4; Matthew 10:34-36).

Recapping the Chapter

What forces drive a pastor's wife to mentally snap and break glass against her bathroom wall? It is the same evil influence that caused an exhausted pastor to consider driving his automobile into the path of an oncoming train. While we cannot lay all the blame at the door of warring factions and church bosses, a good deal of the responsibility may be placed there.

Church history reveals that persecution from without only makes the church stronger and brings about growth; but persecution from within is a destroying influence.[2] The devil hates the church. If he cannot destroy it by feeding its sheep to the lions, he will try feeding its shepherds to the sheep—the ones with long pointy ears and bushy tails and sharp teeth.

This book is not about bitterness or sour grapes. It is about surviving and thriving in the face of opposition and learning how to be at peace while sitting at the Father's banquet table in the very presence of the enemy.

2

Double Agents Unaware

W hen someone goes looking for evidence, there is a presumption that a crime has been committed. The criminal almost always leaves little telltale signs that on closer examination lead to the identification of the perpetrator. The havoc church bosses inflict on the body of Christ, and in particular the pastor and his family, is nothing short of a crime. The fingerprints of their disruptive behavior is evident from Genesis to Revelation. This chapter tracks the evidence of the existence and practices of church bosses as they are exposed in Scripture. The identification of some of the perpetrators may surprise you. Some were very open in their rebellion while others were agents for the dark side without being aware of it themselves. For our purposes, we shall call this latter group "double agents unaware."

Recently, the news media has been abuzz with talk of double agents who work for foreign governments and successfully steal some of our most sensitive military secrets. Spies are dangerous people who slip into top-secret installations and pass information to their respective governments. We have spies and so do all the developed nations of the so-called civilized world. It is a messy but necessary business.

The church is in spiritual warfare. The archenemy of the church has agents among us who not only steal our most sensitive information, but they disrupt communications, discourage leaders or assassinate their character or reputation, seduce key people to destroy their testimonies, and sow discord among the brethren (see Proverbs 6:14, 19). Many times these agents in the church do not even realize they are being used by the dark side. They are double agents unaware.

When I came to the sad conclusion that good people are sometimes used for evil purposes, I searched the Scriptures to find proof. The evidence was not difficult to locate. I discovered that unlike the traitor Judas or the deserter Demas, there were people who believed they were doing God a favor by their sinful behavior. Their fingerprints of spiritual espionage are in both the Old and New Testaments.

Old Testament Agents Unaware

Eve. Genesis 3 tells of the seduction of Eve by the serpent. Once she believed his story, she immediately gave the forbidden fruit to her husband. She probably believed she was actually doing him a favor. After all, now they would be as gods, knowing the difference between good and evil (vv. 1-7).

If Eve had known of the great misery she was bringing on future generations, she would not have listened to the serpent nor tempted her husband to also rebel against God's commandment. With her decision came all manner of sickness and disease, sorrow and heartache and, eventually, death for her and the whole human family. No mother would knowingly bring such misery on her children. The havoc she caused resounds even to our generation. Since there was no organized church at that time, Eve would be our first shadow or type of a church boss. She used her considerable influence with her husband to seduce him to rebel against the Creator. Generations later Jesus would warn His followers:

> Think not that I am come to send peace on earth: I came not to send peace, but a sword. For I am come to set a man at variance against his father, and the daughter against her mother, and the daughter in law against her mother in law. And a man's foes shall be they of his own household (Matthew 10:34-36).

Job's wife. Some scholars consider the Book of Job to be the oldest book in the Bible. If this is true, then Job's wife would be the next double agent unaware. Oh, she was not alone. Job's "friends" also served in that role; but she was in a position to have the most influence on him.

If you want to threaten a woman, take away her security. Job's wife had grown accustomed to living well. Job was the Bill Gates of his day—the richest man of his generation. He lost his wealth, health, and children all in a brief period of time. Sitting among the ashes scraping his running sores with a broken piece of pottery, his wife said he should just curse God and die.

She meant well. Job was a broken man, and she thought this would at least get him out of his misery. She was sincere, but she was sincerely wrong. What if she had convinced Job to forsake God in a time of adversity? Generations of believers would have never been blessed by this story of great victory—Job's restoration of wealth, health and family (see Job 2:10; 42:12-17).

The 10 spies. In the Book of Numbers we read the account of the 12 spies Moses sent to search out the land of Canaan. Each man selected was a ruler among his people, the head of a clan. They spent 40 days searching the land, collecting samples of available food supplies, and evaluating the defense systems of the armies Israel would encounter.

When they returned, 10 of the 12 gave a very negative report. Only two, Joshua and Caleb, said, "Let us go up at once, and possess it; for we are well able to overcome it" (Numbers 13:30).

The naysayers meant well. They thought they were preserving their people from certain disaster; but in the process, they discouraged a nation and sidetracked the fulfilling of God's promises for 40 years. After this, the children of Israel could not enter the Promised Land until every male of fighting age (20 years and older) had perished in the wilderness. The 10 spies were double agents unaware. The nation of Israel was a shadow or type of the church and Moses was the pastor.

David's brothers. The prophet Samuel relates the next example of double agents unaware—David's older brothers (1 Samuel 17). It may help us to understand why God did not choose one of them as king, especially Eliab the eldest.

Saul and his army had been facing the Philistines for 40 days across the valley of Elah. Each day the Philistine champion, Goliath, came out and taunted the armies of Israel. Jesse, David's father, sent him down to the battlefield to check on his three brothers—Eliab, Abinadab and Shammah. While there, David heard the threats of the Philistine and inquired about Saul's promise of rewards to the man who would fight and kill Goliath. David's oldest brother, Eliab, overheard David's inquires and rebuked him.

Eliab first questioned David's motives for even being present at the battle.Then he belittled David's importance to the war effort. Fortunately, his brother's comments did not discourage David in the least.

Satan still uses this same tactic on us today. He first questions our calling.Then he belittles our importance.

Had Eliab succeeded in discouraging his little brother that day, Israel would not have won a great victory over their enemy, and generations of us would not have heard how a little boy with only a sling and stone overcame impossible odds to become the king of Israel and the ancestor of the Lord Jesus. Since David became the progenitor of the founder of the church, his brothers—especially Eliab—became shadows or types of church bosses who would appear later in New Testament and modern times. Are we beginning to see a pattern? Church bosses speak discouraging words to persons in leadership roles.

Cain. All shadows and types of church bosses who appeared in the Old Testament were not agents unaware. Some knew very well what they were doing. Cain, for example, wanted dominion over his brother, Abel. This is the basic motive behind most church bosses. God even warned Cain that sin was "crouching" at his door and gave him an opportunity to repent. But the day came when Cain invited his brother into the field with evil intent in his heart to murder him (see Genesis 4:1-8).

Judas was Cain's equivalent in the New Testament. Once Judas resolved in his heart to betray the Lord Jesus, he proceeded toward his dark destiny with purpose and determination to its tragic conclusion. In the end, he heard the siren voice of the great deceiver inviting him to a tree with a rope in his hand (see Matthew 27:2-5).

New Testament Agents Unaware

Simon Peter. The apostle Peter is our first candidate for a double agent unaware in the New Testament. Both Matthew and Mark relate the story of Peter's rebuke of Jesus when He said He must go to Jerusalem to suffer and die and be resurrected. Peter had just made his great confession that Jesus was the Christ, the Son of the living God. He could not reconcile in his mind that Christ was to suffer and die at the hands of men. He pulled Jesus aside and rebuked Him for His statements.

Peter thought he was doing Jesus a favor by discouraging Him from submitting to such treatment. Peter did not realize Satan was using him to dissuade Jesus from His preordained destiny. Jesus, however, immediately recognized the source of the statement and turned to His good friend and rebuked him.

Remember, Satan had been unsuccessful in tempting Jesus in the desert when he approached Him directly (see Matthew 4). Now he tempted Him through Peter, His good friend and confidant.

Beware of good friends who try to discourage you from fulfilling God's purpose for your life. They may be double agents unaware. Even though they mean well and may even think they are doing you a favor, you must carefully weigh their advice. Especially beware of discouraging voices. Church bosses can come from the ranks of your close friends.

The Judaizers. Paul had two groups of double agents who caused him grief. The first group was the Judaizers. These men from Jerusalem came to Paul with letters of recommendation from the brethren. They tried to shackle Paul's new Gentile coverts with Jewish legalism, saying that one could not become a Christian without first becoming a Jewish proselyte. Paul fought this false doctrine with all his spiritual and mental strength. He referred to them as false brethren who came to secretly spy on the liberty among the Gentiles (Galatians 2:4). They thought they were preserving the traditions of the fathers and saw themselves as the "keepers of the faith." In reality, they were making the death and resurrection of Jesus ineffective by preaching that one could not be saved by faith alone. These men were dangerous double agents. In fact, Paul had no problem identifying them as representatives of the dark side. The next group, however, were much more subtle and difficult to identify as double agents.

The elders from Ephesus. Paul was on his way to Jerusalem, where he would begin his long ordeal that would eventually lead him to Nero's chopping block. When his ship docked at Miletus, he sent for the elders of the church at Ephesus to meet with him for a final time of fellowship and instruction.

Consider who these men were. They were leaders in the church at Ephesus, handpicked by Paul to take care of the flock in his absence. Paul had two concerns. First, that these leaders would let down their guard and allow "grievous wolves" to slip in among them and plunder the flock without mercy. But the most surprising revelation is found in his next statement: "Also of your own selves shall men arise, speaking perverse things, to draw disciples after them" (Acts 20:30).

Was Paul just a good student of human nature? Did he have reason to suspect some of these men of sedition, or had the Holy Spirit revealed these things to him? What we do know is that his predictions came true. He would later write to these men from prison with additional admonitions.

What does this whole scenario have to do with our search for local church bosses in the New Testament? Paul's young protégé, Timothy, later became the pastor of the church at Ephesus and some of his mentor's predictions came true while he was there. Two men, Hymenaeus and Alexander, rose up in rebellion against the young pastor. Paul delivered them to Satan long-distance from his prison cell so they "might learn not to blaspheme" (1 Timothy 1:20).

In the first few verses of Revelation 2, John the Revelator gives us a final look at the church at Ephesus. They had followed Paul's advice, "trying them which say they are apostles and are not, and found them liars" (v. 2). But somewhere along the line, they had fallen out of love with Jesus (v. 4). This offense was so grievous to God that He threatened to come and remove their candlestick if they did not repent and do their first works over (v. 5). Of all the things we do to offend a holy God, nothing is as offensive as "leaving our first love." Becoming a double agent for the other side is as simple as falling out of love with Jesus. Maybe this gives us insight into why some people become church bosses. They become so involved working for God that they fall out of love with Him.

Double Agents in the Mirror

Have you ever been a double agent unaware? Almost all of us have been at one time. We acted in this capacity when we criticized the length of the pastor's sermon in the presence of our spouse and children on the way home from church. Years later we wondered why our young adult children were not interested in church and when they did attend, they were very critical of almost everything. Where did this critical attitude come from? It came from us while they were growing up.

We were double agents unaware when we spoke words of fear and doubt as the pastor tried to cast his vision for the local church. As double agents we voted "no" on the financing of new outreach ministries and programs. We justified our behavior by reasoning, "We're being good stewards of the church's resources." So while looking for double agents unaware in Scripture, we must not forget to look in the mirror. It is like the comic strip character, Pogo, who once said: "We have met the enemy and he is us."[1]

Recapping the Chapter

Not all double agents unaware and shadows and types

of church bosses succeeded in confusing and disrupting the people of God in their efforts to build the Kingdom.

- Eve succeeded all too well, but Job's wife did not.

- The 10 spies in Moses' day delayed but did not stop the fulfillment of God's promises to Israel.

- David's brother Eliab did not discourage him from fulfilling his destiny.

- The apostle Peter could not stop Jesus from going to Jerusalem to face the cross.

- Paul's antagonists are still with us today, trying to chain the church to legalistic traditions that have nothing to do with heartfelt salvation. They are having limited success but appear to be a dying breed.

We might conclude that local church bosses are rather successful in hindering and delaying the work of the Lord, but they are much less successful in bringing it to a screeching halt. This is little consolation, however, to those who have to deal with them on a daily basis. After we spend a little more time in the next chapter identifying these who disrupt your congregation, an attempt will be made to provide you with some practical tools to level the playing field. Then let the games begin.

3

Profiling the Local Church Boss

Sometimes pastors feel they are in a game of masquerade, because local church bosses come in all shapes, sizes, genders and political persuasions. Some come as wolves in sheep's clothing and a few even show up disguised as angels of light.

The reason the Vietcong gave the United States such a hard time in Vietnam was because the Americans could not tell "friendlies" from "unfriendlies." Pastors have the same problem. They have a difficult time distinguishing between the good guys and the bad guys—especially when the bad guys dress in their Sunday best and sit on the front pew. This chapter is designed to help the shepherd tell the sheep from the goats and the wolves.

Some years ago the FBI realized that certain criminals are distinguishable and have somewhat predictable behavioral characteristics. They called this new police procedure of characterizing these criminals *profiling,* and NBC produced a popular television series by the same name. Local church bosses have a certain profile that helps us identify them.

How does the pastor identify church bosses without becoming overly analytical and paranoid? Sometimes the task is amazingly simple. Either the church bosses will divulge their identity, or former pastors will leave tearstains on the parsonage carpet near a suicide note identifying their antagonists by name.

Wolves Who Masquerade as Sheep

Wolves in the Bible are described as predators who kill and devour without mercy. The prophet Ezekiel characterized the leaders of Israel in such a manner: "Her princes in the midst thereof are like wolves ravening the prey, to shed blood, and to destroy souls, to get dishonest gain" (22:27).

The prophet Habakkuk referred to the Babylonian army as being "more fierce than the evening wolves" (1:8). And the prophet Zephaniah used this same terminology to identify the corrupt judges of Israel (3:3).

As Jesus was ending His Sermon on the Mount, He gave the first important clue on how to identify wolves disguised as sheep: "Beware of false prophets, which come to you in sheep's clothing, but inwardly they are ravening wolves. Ye shall know them by their fruits" (Matthew 7:15, 16).

In this same sermon Jesus had said, "Judge not, that ye be not judged" (7:1). On the surface, this statement appears to be in conflict with Christ's advice in verses 15 and 16. But if Jesus did not see it as a conflict, neither should we. Wolves dressed as sheep in our congregation are dangerous predators! If we can identify them by their fruits (as outlined in Galatians 5), we are ahead of the game.

Inspecting the Fruit

Jesus said if a man wanted to harvest grapes, he would not go to a thornbush; or if he wanted figs, he would not gather them from thistles (Matthew 7:16-18). If we use the fruit of the Spirit and the fruit of the flesh given in Galatians 5 as a checklist, we can screen people disguised as wolves and angels of light. Their true identities can be revealed.

For example, have you ever noticed that church bosses are always in a bad mood? It appears as though they wake up every morning thinking, *What can I be unhappy about today?* They come to the church office with a chip on their shoulder and dump their daily load of negative trivia at the pastor's door. Then they go away feeling somewhat better for the moment because it is cathartic for them. Meanwhile, the pastor has to carry their burdens for the rest of the day. Such people have lost their joy in Jesus, not to mention peace of mind—two of the good fruits.

The second clue is the tone of voice they use with the pastor. It is usually gruff and demanding. This is certainly not the voice of a meek person who is filled with goodness and long-suffering. The voice of the wolf is guttural and snarling, while the sheep has a gentle voice. Wolves growl, especially when struck by the truth in the Shepherd's staff.

Even though wolves dress up like sheep, it is impossible for them to behave or sound like sheep. The growls and aggressive behavior give them away every time.

Wolves, Serpents and Doves

Jesus gave His followers additional advice on how to deal with wolves. When He sent the Twelve out to evangelize, He said, "Behold, I send you forth as sheep in the midst of wolves: be ye therefore wise as serpents, and harmless as doves" (Matthew 10:16). Luke substituted the word *lambs* for *sheep* when reporting the same event (Luke 10:3), indicating the vulnerability of the little lambs among ravenous wolves. The only way we can survive is with divine wisdom as harmless messengers of the Word.

In a bare-knuckled fist fight between a sheep and a wolf, the wolf will win every time. Until a person has pastored a church, he probably thinks Jesus was referring to wolves "outside" the church. Not necessarily so.

Falling Out of Love With Jesus

John the Revelator provides the last look at the church in Ephesus. They had been faithful in good works, but they had lost their first love (Revelation 2:1-4). Becoming a local church boss may be as tragically simple as falling out of love with the Founder of the church, or becoming so busy working for God they forget to love God. Pastors can fall into this same trap.

So, how do pastors identify the wolves who masquerade as sheep? If we follow the Chief Shepherd's advice, we will first examine their fruit. Next, as pastors, we should pray for divine wisdom and insight so we can remain "wise as serpents and harmless as doves" (Matthew 10:16).

Finally, there is the test of love. Do the sheep love the shepherd, or do they appear to be full of bitterness and hatred?

Angels of Light

Those who come to church masquerading as angels of light fall into two categories. One group is relatively harmless. These are the "super saints" described below. The second group is much more dangerous and sinister. Paul described them in 2 Corinthians 11:13-15:

> For such are false apostles, deceitful workers, transforming themselves into the apostles of Christ. And no marvel; for Satan himself is transformed into an angel of light. Therefore it is no great thing if his ministers also be transformed as the ministers of righteousness; whose end shall be according to their works.

Angels of light are the "super saints" in the church. The pastor is not so concerned that they might not make it to heaven, but that they might "overshoot" the gate. While pastors need all the volunteers they can get, this group will "help" the pastor to death! They are the first to volunteer for anything that appears on the church calendar, and they constantly want to start new ministries—without regard for resources to finance them.

This group will almost always be the first to show up at a called prayer meeting. In fact, they may call the prayer meeting themselves, at an inconvenient time for the pastor, so they can vilify him later for being unspiritual and not attending.

My advice to pastors is to never become a slave to prayer meetings called by others. Join in when your schedule allows, but have your own daily prayer and devotional time. Inform the congregation of your private time so members will only disturb you in an emergency.

If church bosses insist on your coming to their prayer meetings, invite them to yours instead. Very few, if any, will show up. Remember, their real goal is to control you and your schedule.

The Judaizers

During most of Paul's ministry, he was plagued by false teachers called "Judaizers." These men followed Paul. After his departure, they would slip in among the people and teach heresy. Their favorite false teaching was that someone must first become a Jewish proselyte before becoming a Christian. This, of course, included being circumcised. Paul carried this battle all the way back to the Jerusalem Council for a definitive answer, and the council exonerated him by the ruling and follow-up letter (see Acts 15).

There is evidence in Scripture, however, that the letter from James did not stop the Judaizers from teaching their false doctrine. They often would become part of a local congregation and be a "thorn in the flesh" (2 Corinthians 12:7) to the appointed pastor. They became church bosses of the most dangerous kind, because they taught heresy and encouraged the people to rebel against the sound doctrine taught by the pastor.

Paul was not very patient with these false teachers. He named two of them, Hymenaeus and Alexander, in his first letter to Timothy, saying he had "delivered [them] unto Satan, that they may learn not to blaspheme" (1 Timothy 1:20). Paul was acting in his apostolic role as overseer of the churches when he took this action, but he was backed by the authority of the church fathers in Jerusalem. Heresy in the church cannot be tolerated.

To combat false teaching in the local church, Paul advised Timothy, "Study to shew thyself approved unto God, a workman that needeth not to be ashamed, rightly dividing the word of truth" (2 Timothy 2:15). Paul also advised him to be "an example of the believers, in word, in conversation, in charity, in spirit, in faith, in purity . . . [and] give attendance to reading, to exhortation, [and] to [sound] doctrine" (1 Timothy 4:12, 13).

How then can a pastor reveal or unmask a church boss who masquerades as an angel of light? How can the pastor expose these church bosses to the congregation for what they really are—deceivers? Paul's advice to Timothy was to keep preaching sound doctrine, letting the Word expose false doctrine and those who taught it. Also, he advised him to be an example of pure living to the congregation. We must always let our personal and professional lives be above reproach.

Other Disguises

While wolves in sheep's clothing and false teachers decked out as angels of light constitute two of the more dangerous elements in the church, there are many other masks worn by local church bosses.

The police inspector. This church boss polices the schedules of the senior pastor and his staff members, making regular rounds of the buildings and grounds to be sure everyone is working and in order. This church boss may also phone the church office several times a day, just to see if the phones are being answered promptly. He is usually sound asleep, however, when the pastor is called in the middle of the night to comfort the family of a dying member . . . or to visit a teenager in jail who has been picked up on drug charges.

The retired minister. You can recognize this local church boss by the way he dresses. His costume consists of a polyester suit and long-sleeved white shirt and tie, which he surely must wear while sleeping and mowing his grass. He constantly reminds the pastor how much better things were in the church's earlier days.

The sweet little ole lady. This church boss just happens to be the best cook in the church. She supplies the pastor with cakes, pies and all his favorite dishes. How could he not then give her special favors an inordinate amount of his time? She seems harmless enough, but if the object is to control the pastor and his schedule, or influence church policy, she can be sweetly dangerous.

Recapping the Chapter

Church bosses come in many shapes and sizes, making them difficult to profile. They may appear as a wolf in sheep's clothing, an angel of light, a police inspector, or a sweet little ole lady. They do, however, have certain common characteristics—they want to control the pastor using various means. Fear, intimidation and bullying form one end of the spectrum . . . pies, cakes and projected guilt make up the other extreme.

4

A Matter of Control

W hat do wife beaters, serial killers, rapists and local church bosses have in common? They all want control of their victims. This chapter looks at "controlling" personalities along with ways and means of dealing with them.

For example, the controlling personality type is someone who is basically insecure. They bring order to their world by dominating or controlling someone or something. Understanding their motive gives the pastor or victim a decided advantage. As James 4:7 says, "Resist the devil, and he will flee from you."

In the popular film *Sleeping With the Enemy*, the story line revolves around a controlling husband who has an obsessive compulsive personality. He mentally abuses his wife by placing unreasonable standards of perfection on her, and when she does not live up to his impossible expectations, he physically abuses her. In the end she shoots him and phones the police to inform them she has just shot an intruder.[1]

Now, let us be clear here. It is not legal, moral, ethical or Biblical to shoot local church bosses . . . even though the thought will cross your mind from time to time! Pastors must gently and firmly wrest control from the few (the church bosses) and give it back to the many (the congregation).

Dr. Tim Kimmel has written an excellent book on controlling personalities, titled *How to Deal With Powerful Personalities*. In it he includes 101 ways to identify and manage a controlling person. This should be required reading for every Bible school student majoring in pastoral ministries. Our working definition of a local church boss is a paraphrase of a statement, by Kimmel, which defines *control* in the following way:

> Control is when you leverage the strength of your position or personality against the weakness of someone else's in order to get that person to meet your selfish agenda.[2]

A basic understanding of why some people have the urge or need to control others can be helpful to pastors. Kimmel says, "Fear, rage and shame fuel a high control personality."[3]

Fear, Rage and Shame

What does Scripture say about *fear, rage* and *shame*?

Solomon said, "The fear of the Lord is the beginning of wisdom: and the knowledge of the holy is understanding" (Proverbs 9:10). Fear in this usage is an awesome respect of a holy God. Fear is good when it is the emotion that warns us of impending danger and prepares us for "fight" or "flight." But what happens when people become over-whelmed with fear in the course of their daily lives? Some have panic attacks and withdraw from society. Others turn into controlling personality types in an attempt to bring order to their world. Local church bosses may be victims of this "toxic fear," as Dr. Kimmel describes it.

It is not God's will for His people to suffer from toxic fear. The apostle Paul said, "For ye have not received the spirit of bondage again to fear; but ye have received the spirit of adoption, whereby we cry, Abba, Father" (Romans 8:15). In writing to Timothy, Paul said, "For God hath not given us the spirit of fear; but of power, and of love, and of a sound mind" (2 Timothy 1:7). John the Beloved said, "There is no fear in love; but perfect love casteth out fear: because fear hath torment. He that feareth is not made perfect in love" (1 John 4:18).

Some local church bosses may be suffering from toxic fear of some unknown origin in their pasts. Perhaps they should be pitied and prayed for so they can be made per-fect (mature) in love. They are tormented souls who seek to bring order to this world by controlling others. Unfortunately, the pastor becomes a target.

Fear is often driven by unrequited anger, which is another strong emotion that functions as a two-edged sword. Anger can be a good thing when it stirs righteous indignation to respond positively. Remember when Jesus looked with anger on the legalists who criticized Him for healing on the Sabbath Day? What about the time He drove the money changers from the Temple? He was angry, and His righteous indignation was tested to its absolute limit. Scripture warns us to be "angry, and sin not" (Ephesians 4:26).

In the original Greek, the word *anger* meant "violent passion, abhorrence, indignation, vengeance, wrath." Local church bosses tend to have a lot of pent-up anger, which they release toward the pastor and his family.

It grieves the Holy Spirit when God's people are angry with each other. Listen to Paul's admonition to the church at Ephesus:

> And grieve not the holy Spirit of God, whereby ye are sealed unto the day of redemption. Let all bitterness, and wrath, and anger, and clamour, and evil speaking, be put away from you, with all malice: And be ye kind one to another, tenderhearted, forgiving one another, even as God for Christ's sake hath forgiven you (Ephesians 4:30-32).

Dr. Kimmel said, "Anger turns toxic when people refuse to show understanding or mercy. . . . When anger is not properly processed, it turns to rage. Rage is anger out of control."[4]

The Scripture has some interesting things to say about rage and its high cost to those who allow their emotions to go unchecked.

- Naaman, the Syrian military commander, raged against the instructions given to him by Elisha and almost missed his healing from the dreaded disease of leprosy (2 Kings 5).

- Sennacherib, the king of Assyria, raged against God's anointed leader, Hezekiah, and lost 185,000 of his troops in one night to an avenging angel (2 Kings 18—20).

- King Asa of Judah raged against the seer God sent

to reprove him, and died a miserable death diseased in his feet (2 Chronicles 16).

■ Nebuchadnezzar, the king of Babylon, raged against the three Hebrew boys and later lost his mind because of his false pride and arrogance (Daniel 2; 4:28-37).

Are we beginning to see a pattern here? Those who lost control of their temper and lashed out against God's anointed leaders suffered great loss. Yet, local church bosses engage in this type of behavior with impunity on a regular basis, as though they are exempt from the wrath of God.

The psalmist said the heathen would even rage against God's anointed Christ (Psalm 2:1, 2). Peter and John later quoted this scripture after their hearing before the Jewish leaders in the Temple (Acts 4:25, 26).

Solomon said that jealousy causes rage in a man (Proverbs 6:34). In the original Greek language, the word *rage* meant "to snort (as a spirited horse); to make a tumult." What pastor has not been disturbed at one time or another by the spirited "snorting" of a local church boss?

In addition to toxic fear and anger, local church bosses are often filled with *shame* from some bygone incident. Perhaps they were abused as children or lost face at home or on the job. In any case, if something or someone victimized them, causing a loss of control, they may be desperately trying to regain their equilibrium by victimizing or controlling others.

Like fear and anger, shame can be a positive force. It forms the basis for legitimate guilt when we have wronged others. It's what Peter felt when he went out and wept bitterly after he had thrice denied the Lord. Later, he and John would rejoice that they had been counted worthy to suffer shame for the name of Jesus when they were flogged and released by the Jewish leaders.

Jesus willingly went to the cross while despising the shame so He might fulfill His destiny and free the world from sin.

On the negative side, Paul spoke of the shame of false teachers and of those who fall away from the faith, crucifying Christ afresh (Hebrews 6:4-6).

Just like fear and anger, God does not want His people controlled by toxic shame. Peter said, "Therefore it is also contained in the scripture, 'Behold, I lay in Zion a chief cornerstone, elect, precious, and he who believes on Him will by no means be put to shame'" (1 Peter 2:6, *NKJV*).

Of all the scriptures that speak on the subject of shame, Jude is the most relentless. The brother of the Lord described the apostates in the church as "certain men crept in unawares" (Jude 4). So these were not outsiders—they were men who had actually attached themselves to the church fellowship:

> These are spots in your feast of charity, when they feast with you, feeding themselves without fear: clouds they are without water, carried about of winds; trees whose fruit withereth, without fruit, twice dead, plucked up by the roots; raging waves of the sea, foaming out their own shame; wandering stars, to whom is reserved the blackness of darkness for ever. . . . These are murmurers, complainers, walking after their own lusts; and their mouth speaketh great swelling words, having men's persons in admiration because of advantage (vv. 12, 13, 16).

Fear, anger and shame lead to bondage. And bondage, Kimmel said, "insists that we control the people around us. If we do not, we leave ourselves vulnerable to their scrutiny and rejection."[5]

While we are looking for these traits in others, we must be careful not to fall into the control trap ourselves. This will be discussed in the next chapter.

A Tale of Two Pastors

Two "control-the-pastor" stories may be useful here. The first involves the account of a senior pastor who was training an intern. The younger man noticed that the senior pastor made a phone call every day at the same time in the early afternoon. The call was to an elderly shut-in, who let the pastor know that he expected a phone call every day at that exact time. The pastor had become a slave to meeting this unreasonable expectation. Worse still, he was teaching the intern to chain himself to the same bondage.

What really was happening was this: an incapacitated church boss was still controlling the pastor from a distance. Let me hasten to say that shut-ins are precious members of the fold who should not be neglected; but pastors should control their own schedules.

The second story also involves a shut-in. This was a sweet lady who expected a visit from her pastor on a certain day of the week . . . *every* week. She chided him if he ever had to delay or cancel a visit. His flock was large (over 1,000 members) and one sheep, however worthy, was demanding a disproportionate amount of his time.

This was a clear case of delegate or regulate. Some possible solutions would be to assign this visit to a staff person or active layman, regulate the schedule to less frequent contact or vary the times of the visits.

Unfortunately, neither of these stories had a happy ending. In the first case, the senior pastor kept phoning at the same time each afternoon and told his intern he should do the same.

In the second case, the senior pastor snapped one day when the woman reprimanded him for missing his scheduled visit. This triggered pent-up rage and frustration in the senior pastor, which eventually led to substance abuse. He finally resigned and lost his ministry. He had tried to do the impossible—be all things to all people.

As much as possible, we must control our schedule. We must not let our schedule control us or others control our schedule.

A Dog's Tale

A friend of mine had a large, gentle-natured collie whom everyone, including the family, just called "Dog." When we visited, Dog would come towards us with head lowered and tail wagging, wanting to be petted. We were always happy to oblige.

Dog had one disturbing characteristic—he was frightened of thunderstorms. When a storm came, Dog would assault the door of his master's house until someone let him inside or the storm passed through the area.

Dog's behavior was predictable. He always ran home during storms, and he always met us in the driveway with a lowered head and wagging tail. Not once during our visits did Dog meet us in the driveway with his tail wagging him.

When local church bosses try to usurp the authority over the pastor, it is much like the tail trying to wag the dog. But let a serious storm come into the life of a church boss, and he will pound on the pastor's door for comfort. Most pastors will kindly let him inside and speak words of comfort until the storm passes by.

Recapping the Chapter

Local church bosses tend to have controlling personalities. They are driven by fear, anger and shame from some unknown origin in their past. Displaced anger is often released toward the pastor and his family.

God does not want His children bound by fear, anger, and toxic guilt or shame. The pastor has a responsibility to pray for these errant, antagonistic members of his flock. It falls into the category of praying for those who "despitefully use you" (Matthew 5:44). Also, the pastor should be on his guard against falling into the control trap himself. This trap is deep and deceptive; large doses of the grace of God are needed to extricate it.

Remember, God never intended for the tail to wag the dog. It is not the divine order of things.

5

Lords Over the Flock

The only thing worse than a local church boss with a controlling personality is a pastor with a controlling personality. The Lord's flock is to be fed and led—not driven and beaten by the shepherd. The apostle Peter warned against such behavior on the part of the shepherd.

Pastors should learn how to be servant leaders, using the apostle Peter as their model. Peter had to learn his shepherding role the hard way. Always the outspoken one, he had a major case of "foot-in-mouth disease." Peter . . .

- Spoke out of confusion and fear on the Mount of Transfiguration.

- Became a "double agent unaware" and tried to discourage the Lord from fulfilling His destiny in Jerusalem.

- Dared to step out of the boat in the middle of a stormy sea to walk on the water to Jesus.

- Refused, at first, to let the Lord wash his feet and then declared he would never forsake Christ, even if all the other disciples did.

- Even in the post-Resurrection period, when Jesus questioned Peter's love and devotion over breakfast on the seashore, Peter wanted to know what John's future held. In today's vernacular, Jesus told Peter, "Mind your own business, do your assignment, and don't worry about John's job description."

Peter's job was to feed the sheep. His was to be a shepherding or pastoring role. Did he finally learn his lesson? Yes, he did. Oh, he still had bouts with racial prejudice, but nobody doubted his commitment after the Day of Pentecost.

By the time he wrote his epistles, Peter was a seasoned warrior, an aging elder with advice to other shepherds. Christian tradition says Peter was executed by crucifixion just outside of Rome—a fate which the Lord had foretold (John 21:18, 19).

Let us analyze the exhortation of Peter to the elders in the churches. What emerges is the image of the servant leader:

> The elders which are among you I exhort, who am also an elder, and a witness of the sufferings of Christ, and also a partaker of the glory that shall be revealed: Feed the flock of God which is among you, taking the oversight thereof, not by constraint, but willingly; not for filthy lucre, but of a ready mind; neither as being lords over God's heritage, but being ensamples to the flock. And when the

chief Shepherd shall appear, ye shall receive a crown of glory that fadeth not away. Likewise, ye younger, submit yourselves unto the elder. Yea, all of you be subject one to another, and be clothed with humility: for God resisteth the proud, and giveth grace to the humble. Humble yourselves therefore under the mighty hand of God, that he may exalt you in due time (1 Peter 5:1-6).

The word *feed* in the original language means "to tend as a shepherd." The word *oversight* means "to oversee, to beware; to look diligently." This describes a shepherd who finds green pastures for the flock and is constantly on alert for predators who may harm the sheep.

The good shepherd serves the sheep, not out of compulsion, for financial gain, or as lords over God's heritage. The good shepherd is a caring example to the flock.

To act as *lords over* means to "control, subjugate; exercise dominion over." The word *heritage* means "an acquisition by inheritance." The word picture painted by the apostle is one of a domineering, abusive shepherd who mistreats the Chief Shepherd's inheritance. Since we are "heirs and joint heirs" with Christ, it would be tantamount to mistreating one's own inheritance.

Furthermore, the younger elders (which is not a contradiction of terms) were to submit themselves to the senior elders. In fact, all the elders were to submit to each other, being "clothed" in humility.

When the Chief Shepherd appears, the elders who did these things would be rewarded with a "crown of glory" that would not fade with time.

Unfortunately, controlling personalities are not just found in the pews—they are in the pulpits as well. Kimmel said, "The prefix *Reverend* before a name is not a license to control other people."[1] Pastors have been called to a leadership role, and opportunities to abuse their position abound. They must resist the temptation to control and manipulate even more than laymen.

While the pulpit certainly should be used for vision casting and moving forward the agenda of the body, it should not be used to bully people or advance personal agendas. If pastors do not want members of their congregations to rise up and "lord" over them, then they should not lord over their members. Servant leaders must lead by example, not coercion.

What was Jesus trying to tell the disciples when He said, "Except ye be converted, and become as little children, ye shall not enter into the kingdom of heaven?" (Matthew 18:3). What was His purpose in telling His disciples that they were not to lead as worldly authorities do, but that the greatest among them must be the servant of all? (23:11).

Perhaps the Lord shared these thoughts with the disciples because they were constantly discussing who should be the greatest among them when the Lord set up His kingdom. The mother of James and John was so bold as to ask the Lord directly for this favor to be shown to her sons (20:20-23).

When the disciples looked to the Jewish temple, they saw a pyramid-type bureaucracy headed by a corrupt high priest. When they looked to the government, they saw a pyramid headed by a corrupt Caesar and supported by a corrupt military. No wonder they were confused when

Jesus said things like, "And whosoever shall compel thee to go a mile, go with him twain" (5:41).

Building on this principle, the writer of Romans advised his readers, "Therefore if thine enemy hunger, feed him; if he thirst, give him drink" (Romans 12:20). On the night before He was crucified, Jesus turned the social order upside-down when He washed the disciples' feet. In the social pecking order of their day, this was the duty of the lowest slave in the household. Yet, just a few hours before He would submit Himself to the will of the Father and the cruel intentions of a corrupt government, Jesus washed His disciples' feet.

The ordinance of "washing the saints' feet" has all but disappeared in the modern church. I challenge you to find its moral equivalent and offer to perform it for the least deserving—the local church boss.

Tommy Tenney tells of an interesting experience he had while pastoring. While praying about a member of his congregation with whom he had a disagreement, he felt a strong impression that he should offer to shine the member's shoes. Resisting at first because the idea sounded so preposterous, he yielded to the prompting of the Spirit, and worked the scenario into a sermon. He invited the brother on stage with him and proceeded to shine his shoes in front of the congregation. The results were predictable. Tears were shed on both sides. The offended brother in turn offered to shine the pastor's shoes. While the whole congregation wept, the conflict was resolved between the two, and great emotional healing took place.

I witnessed the catharsis that took place in a large auditorium where this story was told. All over the building, people were weeping. Dozens dropped to their knees and began to wipe the dust from each other's shoes, using handkerchiefs, napkins, or whatever pieces of cloth or paper they could find.

In another true story, a pastor with a congregation numbering in the thousands told of a disagreement he had with one of his members that caused tension. In prayer, the pastor was impressed to go to the brother, take the full blame for the disagreement and beg forgiveness. Like Evangelist Tommy Tenney, the pastor at first resisted, but finally yielded his will to God's will.

He called a meeting with the offended brother and took a couple of witnesses so there would be no misunderstanding or misquotes later. At the meeting, the pastor fell on his knees, took full blame for the disagreement and begged for his brother's forgiveness.

This story did not immediately yield the same results as the shoeshine story. The offended brother did not melt in the pastor's arms and assume his portion of the blame. He did not even offer forgiveness; but sometime later when there was a life-threatening illness in his family, he called for the pastor to come and minister to the family. This was his way of saying, "All is well between us."

The Role of the Shepherd

In addition to the feeding and overseeing roles outlined by Peter, the Scriptures are replete with instructions and admonitions regarding the role of the shepherd.

For example, there is that tender moment following the reconciliation between Jacob and Esau. Esau tried to convince his younger brother, Jacob, to press ahead with his flocks and herds. Jacob's response shows his great wisdom and skill as a shepherd. He refused to push the flock faster than its endurance level (see Genesis 33:11-14). Pastors cannot push their congregations beyond their ability or willingness to move. There is a vast difference between leading and driving the sheep.

Psalm 23 is a commentary on the role of the shepherd. In this psalm we see the shepherd leading, restoring, comforting, feeding and anointing. We never see the shepherd pushing, beating or abusing the flock.

Ezekiel 34 should be read very carefully by all those who feel called into pastoral ministry. Ezekiel prophesied against the irresponsible shepherds of Israel because they were . . .

- Feeding themselves while starving the flock

- Failing to strengthen the weak and tend the sick

- Neglecting to search for the lost members of the flock

- Ruling with force and cruelty

- Leaving the flock to the slaughter of the predators.

Because of this gross neglect, God himself said He would seek for His scattered flock and gather them to safety. The irresponsible shepherds would be disinherited and would no longer live well at the expense of the sheep.

In his book *Becoming a Shepherd*, Oliver McMahan said, "Shepherds who abuse their sheep may be tolerated for a time, but eventually they will be cut off from access to the congregation and ministry."

Dale Tar, a well-known seminary president, once said,

"If you do not like the smell of sheep, do not become a shepherd."

Jesus compared Himself, the Good Shepherd, to the hireling who cares nothing for the sheep and runs away at the first sign of danger:

> I am the good shepherd: the good shepherd giveth his life for the sheep. But he that is an hireling, and not the shepherd, whose own the sheep are not, seeth the wolf coming, and leaveth the sheep, and fleeth: and the wolf catcheth them, and scattereth the sheep (John 10:11, 12).

Even if you are a pastor who works for a salary, you should never be guilty of being a hireling who runs away when threatened by a predator—even when the predator emerges from "inside" the flock.

Recapping the Chapter

Pastors should always take the high road. They will never regret it. "When reviled, revile not again" (see 1 Peter 2:23).

Resist the temptation to "lord" over the flock. If you fall into this control trap, you have not risen morally or ethically above your antagonist.

The Lord is looking for servant leaders, so be one. Serve not out of constraint or personal gain—serve willingly.

6

The Corporate Church

L ocal church bosses attempt to usurp the pastor's authority when there is a real or perceived leadership vacuum in the church. This game might be called a "corporate takeover" and is sometimes a "hostile takeover."

How does the pastor prevent this leadership vacuum? This question becomes even more intriguing when we remember the Lord wants servant leaders. By definition the servant leader might be mistakenly viewed as weak and inefficient—an ideal person for a hostile takeover.

First, meekness should not be confused with weakness. Moses, the meekest man of his generation, successfully led a rebellious group of murmuring malcontents through the desert for 40 years.

Jesus was the meekest man on earth, even once described as One who would not snuff out a candle or bruise a reed (Matthew 12:20). Yet He overturned the money changers' tables and drove them forcibly from the Temple.

A servant leader is weak only when he abandons his leadership role. A pastor doesn't have to be an expert in management theory and practice; however, he should have a basic knowledge of how to handle people.

Corporate Model of Management Theory and Practice

When we look at the business world, we find useful models and leadership styles, but nothing really fits the servant-leader role Jesus advocated.

Laurence J. Peter, for example, developed the "Peter Principle." This concept is based on the idea that the corporate world promotes individuals until they reach the level of incompetence. At this point frustration sets in, and the individuals either continue to try to function in a position over their heads or they ask to be relieved of their duties.[1] Pastors often find themselves in this dilemma.

In the '60s and '70s, *Management by Objectives* (MBOs) became popular.[2] This idea seemed to work well in the business world where there were task-oriented supervisors and administrators. The idea even alluded to democratic management, because the objectives were constructed by the employee and supervisor working together in a planning session. MBOs provided a good tool for employee evaluation, because each employee was evaluated on the basis of goal achievement.

In the '80s and '90s, the concept of total quality management was the hot topic of management seminars. This idea was borrowed from Japanese business and industry. It is based on the idea that manufacturing processes should be so precise that no defective products would ever reach the customer.[3] Having no errors or mistakes is a wonderful theory, but as long as human beings are involved, there will be errors, mistakes and deviations from the standard operating procedure. That is why God created grace.

Jesus-the Founder and CEO of the Corporate Church

The New Testament church operated in an environment where the Founder and CEO of the organization got down on His hands and knees one evening and washed the feet of the "board of directors." When one board member refused, he was told he must submit or no longer have a role in the "organization." The board member quickly yielded his will to the Founder and CEO.

This would be somewhat like Bill Gates, the founder and CEO of the highly successful Microsoft Corporation, calling a meeting of his board of directors and getting down on his hands and knees to shine their shoes. Surely their first thought would be that he had lost his mind. In their view it would be highly irrational.

In the church world, the leader must be the servant of all. This is the bureaucratic pyramid of the business world turned upside down. The pastor must never forget who he really works for—a Jewish Carpenter who became a miracle-working, itinerant preacher and changed the status quo without firing a shot in anger. Jesus also is the major stockholder in the organization. He purchased His shares with His own blood, sweat and tears.

Moses–One-Man Show to Delegator

Moses, the lawgiver, kept a crowded court docket in his role as judge. He would hear cases from morning to night. Fortunately, Moses had a wise father-in-law named Jethro. On a visit to his overworked son-in-law, Jethro observed the long hours Moses was sitting in the judgment seat. He made an organizational recommendation that greatly benefitted Moses. Why not select capable God-fearing men to share the burden of judging (see Exodus 18)?

Moses followed his father-in-law's advice and appointed lower court judges over the population. The new court system had five levels. Moses heard only the most difficult cases. What a blessing! Now Moses could spend quality time with his family. (Pastors, take note.) This was the first recorded case of delegation.

In the New Testament era, Jesus selected 12 men and poured Himself into them for over three years. He did, however, teach them some new management skills that were totally foreign to their thinking.

For example, they were not to rule or manage like the Gentiles—an obvious reference to the Roman government. This bit of management consulting advice was given just after the mother of James and John lobbied Jesus for two cabinet positions for her two sons in the new administration. The other disciples were outraged.

> But Jesus called them unto him, and said, Ye know that the princes of the Gentiles exercise dominion over them, and they that are great exercise authority upon them. But it shall not be so among you: but whosoever will be great among you, let him be

your minister; and whosoever will be chief among you, let him be your servant: even as the Son of man came not to be ministered unto, but to minister, and to give his life a ransom for many (Matthew 20:25-28).

This new organization, called the church, was to be run by servant leaders. Unlike the Roman government headed by a corrupt politician claiming to be a god, the church would be founded by a man who was God. And all those who served with Him were to be subject to each other.

The challenge is to be a strong, servant leader—this is not a contradiction of terms. The pastor must be meek without appearing to be weak. Perceived weakness creates a power vacuum, which a strong-willed local church boss will jump into with both feet. The following is a partial list of men and women who appeared weak and vulnerable but changed the world by their quiet determination:

- Jesus was a servant leader, but when the money changers in the Temple needed an object lesson in honesty, they got one (Matthew 21:12-17; Mark 11:15-18).

- Paul was a servant leader, but when it was necessary to exercise his apostolic authority, he could do so.

- James, the brother of the Lord, was a servant leader, but he knew how to combine works with faith to get the job done. He was the one who said, "Resist the devil, and he will flee from you" (James 4:7). To which one church leader I know responded, "But try to resist the church boss and he will stick to you [like glue]."

■ John the Beloved was a man of peace who espoused brotherly love, but he had strong words for a local church boss named Diotrephes (3 John 9).

■ Jude, another brother of the Lord, was a servant leader, but he delivered a seething condemnation of certain men who had "crept in unawares" and were wreaking havoc in the church (Jude 4).

■ Ghandi, closer to our time, brought the British Empire to its knees and cast off the yoke of their control over his nation through his quiet resistance.[4] It took George Washington and the colonial army several years to accomplish this same feat with musket and bayonet.

■ Rosa Parks, a black lady from Alabama, refused to go to the back of the bus reserved for people of her race. Her quiet, dignified courage sparked the conscience of a nation and questioned, "Do we believe in our own constitution, which guarantees certain inherent rights to all citizens?"[5]

Evil will eventually fall of its own weight because it is rotten to the core; it is not built on a firm foundation. We watched in amazement as the Berlin Wall, which had long been a symbol of communist oppression, dismantled before our very eyes. The quiet resistance of the millions trapped behind that wall finally prevailed.

I attended college with a young man from Texas who took great pride in his physical strength. He loved to lift weights and do push-ups on his fingertips. He often won weight lifting contests, but he was not much of a wrestler.

His superior strength could be neutralized by a weaker but quicker opponent.

One evening he came into the dorm room and, in a playful but menacing mood, charged at me. I let him use his superior strength to push me backward onto the bed. Then grabbing both his hands and placing my feet in the pit of his stomach, I flipped him over the bed and slammed him into the wall on the other side of the room. He held me in much more respect after that incident. He was stronger, but my speed and agility had beaten his brute strength.

One thing pastors can count on is the aggressive behavior of the local church boss. They often charge like a mad bull chasing the red cape . . . and you know how that story usually ends. The truth of the Word is in our hands, and it is "sharper than any two-edged sword" (Hebrews 4:12, *NKJV*).

Management Theory and Practice–the Century at a Glance

In 1887, a 31-year-old college professor named Woodrow Wilson suggested that administration should be studied as a separate subject, but it would be 40 more years before the first textbook appeared.[6]

In 1911, Frederick W. Taylor published *Principles of Scientific Management*, a structured management style that emphasized close supervision of factory workers to ensure a low cost per unit on the production line. This type of thinking ushered in the "Era of Scientific Management," which fueled the think tanks of business and industry from 1910-1935.[7]

After the collapse of the stock market in 1929, the business community realized that workers were motivated by more than paychecks. The progressive Western Electric Company conducted some now famous research during this period that led to the so-called human relations movement, which kept management consultants busy from 1935-1950.[8]

From the '50s to the present, the business community has evolved from a postindustrial period into the "information age." Fifty years ago, who could have guessed that a large percentage of homes would have personal computers with Internet links all over the world? The face of business and industry is changing.

Toward the New Century

Not everyone was caught off guard by the changes in business, industry and society in general. In 1990 John Naisbitt and Patricia Aburdene published a national bestseller called *Megatrends 2000: Ten New Directions for the 1990's*. The authors made 10 major predictions for the '90s, most of which materialized:

- A booming global economy

- A Renaissance in the arts

- The emergence of free-market socialism

- Global lifestyles and cultural nationalism

- The privatization of the welfare state

- The rise of the Pacific Rim

- Women in leadership

- The age of biology

- Religious revival of the third millennium

- Triumph of the individual.[9]

It is an exciting time to be alive and view history in the making. The 20th century saw man advance from the horse and carriage to the Saturn V rocket, which was set on a course to the surface of the moon. No other 100-year period in the history of mankind has witnessed so many scientific and technological changes.

Looking forward into the 21st century, the only constant we can count on is change itself. The church must find more innovative ways to minister.

Why are we taking the time to discuss the corporate world and scientific and technological innovation in the middle of a book about *Games Local Church Bosses Play?* Because one of the main attributes of church bosses is their resistance to change.

Could modern-day captains of industry survive in a highly competitive marketplace if they did not stay sensitive to changing customer demands? The answer is a resounding no—they would soon be out of business.

Yet, many churches today operate much the same way that they did 50 or 100 years ago. They sing the same songs, go through the same rituals, and chain themselves to traditions that have almost nothing to do with heartfelt salvation.

Why is this true, when many churches are blessed with young, creative, innovative pastors? It is true because local church bosses sit astride the path of progress, anchor themselves in place, and refuse to allow the church to move beyond their narrow concepts. The Lord never intended for His church to become a museum—He designed it to be a breeding ground for change and innovation.

If we could take only one idea from the corporate world to help the church survive and thrive in a modern society, let it be this: Change is not only inevitable—it is absolutely necessary in order to survive. Local church bosses, however well-intentioned, must not be allowed to stifle constructive innovative change.

Recapping the Chapter

Moses' father-in-law, Jethro, taught one of the first management consultant seminars by helping his busy son-in-law learn the fine art of delegation. During the New Testament era, Jesus taught His disciples to become servant leaders.

Servant leaders may be perceived as weak and inefficient, but meekness and weakness are not the same thing. The Bible is replete with examples of servant leaders who were by no means weak or inefficient.

Over the past century, management theory and practices have gone through a process of change.

The only thing that is constant in the 21st century is change itself. In order to survive and thrive in a changing society, the church must engage in innovative change.

By their very nature, local church bosses are against change. They must not be allowed to usurp the authority of the pastor and affect a "hostile takeover" of the corporate church if the church is to survive and thrive in the 21st century.

7

The Church
Business
Meeting

Church bosses are at their best in church business meetings, where they have an audience for their antics. They enjoy confronting the pastor face-to-face on insignificant matters that are troubling them at the moment. This chapter will suggest strategies to help the pastor counter (without malice) and disarm the antagonist.

In his lectures, John Maxwell tells about being a newly appointed pastor. He asked the head of his church board what they expected of him. He was informed that the pastor's role was to open their business meeting with prayer, close with prayer, and leave the business of the church to the board.

After taking a tour of buildings and grounds, Maxwell made a list of much-needed and long-neglected improvements to the property. Remembering his limited role in board meetings, at first he was frustrated in trying to get these items on the agenda. Then an idea came to him.

Since the head of the church board was a farmer, the pastor decided to spend a day with him on the farm, helping with menial tasks. As they worked side by side, Maxwell casually mentioned the items on his list, without even suggesting that these matters be discussed at the next business meeting. When the meeting convened, the pastor opened with prayer and turned the session over to the chairman. You guessed it. Every item the pastor had mentioned on the farm was presented to the board and was subsequently passed. The pastor closed with prayer and the business meeting adjourned. For the remainder of his tenure at that church, Maxwell opened and closed with prayer and let the chairman push forward his agenda.

While John Maxwell hesitates to call this method of *laissez-faire* management *manipulation,* it is difficult to find a better word for it. Charm and charisma can manipulate others into getting things done. Although this is an effective management tool, it has one serious drawback— it leaves the church boss still enthroned in his position, even encouraging and rewarding his behavior. What happens when a serious issue comes up and the pastor finds himself in total opposition to the position taken by the church boss? Since the pastor has already abdicated his leadership position, there is little chance his position on the matter will receive serious consideration.

In a business meeting I heard of, a pastor was accosted by a church boss and informed that his wife had no business spending donated hours in the church office. She should stay home and mind her own business. He failed to add "and bake cookies," but that was the tone of his voice.

Since the pastor's wife had left a good paying job to donate her time to the church, this abrupt admonition came as quite a shock to the pastor. His response was to advise his wife to seek employment outside the church since her donated time was not appreciated. She followed her husband's advice and faired much better mentally, emotionally and financially. So, in a way, the mean-spirited church boss did the pastor's family a favor, even though the clerical business of the church went lacking.

What does the Bible have to say regarding the pastor's role in church business sessions? The Jerusalem Council, which is recorded in Acts 15:1-31, gives us insight into how the first-century church conducted business.

The Jerusalem Council

"Certain men" had come from Judea and taught in the local churches founded by Paul and Barnabas. The doctrine they espoused was an old covenant concept. Gentiles, they said, could not become Christians unless they first became Jewish proselytes through circumcision. When Paul and Barnabas disagreed with these teachers, a delegation went to Jerusalem for an official resolution. Paul, Barnabas and others went to Jerusalem to meet with the apostles and elders.

When there had been "much disputing," Peter stood up and declared how God had first used him to bring the gospel to the Gentiles. James, who was evidently monitoring the meeting, heard the evidence from both sides and ruled in favor of the liberal views of Paul and Barnabas. The council sent a letter to all the churches ,declaring that Gentiles did not have to first become Jewish proselytes to receive Christ. It was a milestone decision that has influenced the church for two millennia.

While the Jerusalem Council represents the universal church, certain principles may apply to local church business meetings.

First, a clergyman—not a layman—monitored the meeting. Second, while all sides were permitted to present their arguments, no vote was taken at the conclusion. The moderator simply made a ruling much like a judge or mediator might do today. Third, once the decision was made, all the local churches were advised and expected to adhere to the new teaching.

Division of Labor in the Early Church

In Acts 6, we see another example of how the early church conducted business. Some Greek widows felt neglected and discriminated against in the daily distribution of food.

The apostles called a meeting of the church body and asked them to select seven qualified men to distribute the food while the clergy gave themselves "continually to prayer, and to the ministry of the word" (v. 4).

This is one of the distinct divisions of labor that we see between the clergy and the laity in the New Testament church. From this time on, there was a distinction between those who ministered the spiritual food and those who administered the beans and potatoes. The lines did blur a little, however, when two of the seven men selected became great preachers of the gospel. Stephen became the church's first martyr and Philip became a great evangelist.

What does this mean for us today? It obviously means

the pastor should play a greater role in church business meetings, not just praying the opening and closing prayers. The one who has his hand on the spiritual pulse of the church should also help set the church's priorities and guide the vision for the future.

The apostles realized the business of the church had to be a cooperative effort between the clergy and the laity. Each has a role to play. It is easy for pastors to become so bogged down in the day-to-day business affairs of the church that they neglect their roles as intercessors and ministers of the Word.

Practical Hints in Conducting Church Business Meetings

1. A good attorney never asks a question if he does not already know the answer. The same could be said for a pastor as he sets the agenda for church business meetings. Assess the support for an issue before placing it on the agenda, and never call for a vote unless the outcome is fairly certain.

2. While no pastor should want a church council or board that just rubber-stamps his agenda items, it is helpful to have people who are generally supportive of the pastor and his vision for the church. Depending on the recruitment and selection process used, it may take time before a new pastor has a governing board that is favorable to his vision. If you are patient, it is worth the wait.

3. Let an angry or upset member of the board vent his feelings. The web he weaves may eventually entrap him.

4. Avoid marathon meetings unless they are absolutely necessary.

5. How church business meetings are conducted will depend on the denomination. In some denominations the pastor moderates the meeting. In others, he is hardly more than a potted plant while others carry on the business of the church. It is difficult to imagine that the Lord intended His anointed leader to be a fern.

6. If the matter is a weighty one and the council or governing board cannot reach consensus, take it before the congregation for resolution.

7. Your pastor's council or governing board will help to make or break you. Select them well and then pour yourself and your vision for the church into them.

8. Concede small points to win the larger, more important ones, but do not trade your integrity for anything.

The Trivia Game

What is truly amazing is the triviality that divides churches. More demons have been evoked over the selection of carpet for the sanctuary than over a thousand pastoral selections. It is truly the small foxes that destroy or spoil the vine (Song of Solomon 2:15).

In a recent interview with an associate pastor of a prominent church, the subject of turnover at the senior pastor level surfaced. The associate, who had survived several changes, revealed surprising results in a study the church had conducted to determine the reasons for this. It was not the salary or benefit package, it was the grinding down of the senior pastor by a relentless barrage of trivia. Jesus warned us about becoming bogged down in trivia, because "sufficient unto the day is the evil thereof" (Matthew 6:34).

Recapping the Chapter

The pastor of a small, medium or large church must learn to itemize, organize, prioritize and delegate to win the game of trivia. All things on the list do not have to be done by you personally. Some things do not need to be done at all. Some need immediate action. Some can be deferred to a more convenient time.

8

The Money Game

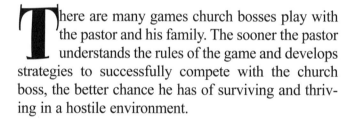

There are many games church bosses play with the pastor and his family. The sooner the pastor understands the rules of the game and develops strategies to successfully compete with the church boss, the better chance he has of surviving and thriving in a hostile environment.

Identifying the Players

The shepherd is the pastor. The sheep are the congregation or flock. The goats travel with the sheep but will be separated in the end. The wolves are predators who sometimes slip in among the sheep.

A noted television evangelist once said, "The pastor should shear the sheep, milk the goats and shoot the wolves." Don't we wish it was that simple? Sometimes we cannot tell the sheep from the goats. That is why God is going to do the separating at the Judgment.

So the pastor may find himself attacked by wolves who disguise themselves as sheep, or attacked by goats who travel with the sheep. This chapter will give the pastor some helpful hints to identify which is which.

It is the nature of a billy goat to butt; he cannot seem to help himself. My family learned this on a vacation trip to Florida.

We were in the petting zoo at Busch Gardens. My wife was carrying a bag of animal food when a small billy goat nudged the bag with his nose and little horns, expecting to be rewarded with food. When he was ignored, he backed off a few paces, lowered his head, and charged full-speed ahead, butting my startled spouse in the thigh. She immediately tossed the bag of food to me and cried, "You feed the animals!"

When a church member is constantly getting upset over trivia and charging the pastor, most likely he is a goat, not a sheep.

Goats have other annoying habits. They climb all over the place and leave their muddy hoofprints. They devour almost anything, including laundry on the clothesline. When members of a congregation tend to go where they have no business and leave their dirty footprints behind, and if they swallow almost anything they come across (including false doctrine), they are probably goats and not sheep.

Wolves present quite a different situation. Goats are a nuisance, but wolves are dangerous—especially the ones who slip in wearing sheep's clothing. Wolves have to be dealt with differently than goats. To test a sheep-looking wolf, nudge it with your staff (the Word). If the response is a growl instead of a baa, you probably have a wolf on your hands.

Even harmless animals can become dangerous. A few years ago, the public was shown a photo of former President Jimmy Carter defending himself with a boat oar against a rabbit with rabies that was attacking his small fishing boat.[1]

Rabbits by nature do not attack people, but this one had become infected with a vicious and fatal virus. So it is with sheep that become infected with rebellion. They sometimes turn against the unsuspecting shepherd. So not only does the shepherd have to stay alert for wolves and goats, but also rabid sheep. Rabies can be passed among animals by eating contaminated food (false doctrine) or a bite from an animal that is already infected. Bites can be fatal even to the shepherd. Keep your staff handy.

The Money Game

The local church boss loves to play the money game because it fits so well with his controlling personality. He gravitates toward anything concerning church finances, including ushering, counting and banking.

The church boss operates from the old adage, "He who controls the purse strings, controls the game." Involvement with church finances gives him a sense of power over the pastor, especially when the church boss and his family are substantial contributors. He may make himself readily available to serve on budget committees, prepare deposits for the bank, or co-sign checks (a favorite) because these functions allow him to review every church expenditure—great or small.

Starve Out

A variation of the money game is "starve out." This is played when the church boss and his friends decide to withhold their tithes and offerings. Sometimes they divert them to other churches or charities, hoping to influence church policy decisions or even determine who the next pastor will be. Players should be cautioned—the tithe portion of their income is holy unto the Lord and it is a dangerous thing to withhold or divert it.

Winning the Money Game

In the secular world, money is synonymous with power, prestige and leverage. It's no surprise that church bosses presume they can use this leverage to advance their agenda. Often a major contributor will take advantage of a situation by trying to influence the pastor or church board to make decisions that may or may not be in the best interest of the congregation.

In the popular musical *Fiddler on the Roof*, the main character is a Russian-born Jewish peasant named Tevye who is preoccupied with the idea of becoming wealthy. He longs to sit with the elders of his people and have those less fortunate come to him for advice. Whether his advice was good or bad, he believes that people would listen if he was rich. All day long he sings to himself, "If I were a rich man."[2]

There is a grain of truth in Tevye's presumptuous thinking. People do tend to take a rich man's advice, whether it is good or bad.

How does the pastor deal with someone who blatantly tries to use his wealth to influence, intimidate and even threaten by withholding contributions? It is not easy, but it can be done.

Jesus had rich friends and enemies, but He was never influenced nor intimidated by them. In fact, He put them in their place by telling His disciples, "It is easier for a camel to go through the eye of a needle, than for a rich man to enter into the kingdom of God" (Matthew 19:24). Many pastors "wine and dine" the wealthy people in their congregation, hoping it will elicit large contributions for worthy church projects. It is OK to have affluent friends and associates—Jesus did. But it's not wise to place all your eggs in one basket. The wealthy usually comprise only a small percentage of the congregation. Any shepherd knows more wool can be obtained from the flock as a whole than from one or two fat sheep, regardless of the fullness of their coats.

In all fairness, not all wealthy people use their income to influence, intimidate or threaten the pastor. Some are faithful to tithe and give with no strings attached.

Paul made tents to support his new-field evangelism. Later, after the churches were established, he gladly accepted offerings from them. Paul even asked one church to forgive him for denying them the privilege of contributing to his ministry (2 Corinthians 12:13).

Another strategy in winning the money game is to learn to rely on the provision of God. This sounds elementary and fundamental, but it is true. Pastors preach from the text "Seek ye first the kingdom of God" (Matthew 6:33), without realizing the promised blessing also applies to them and their churches.

When a small group of members became upset and decided to withhold and divert their tithes, one pastor remained faithful and asked God to provide for the church. Over a three-year period, each time the church income and output were calculated, the church was "in the black" by 1 percent. This could not have happened by chance. In His mercy to this faithful pastor, God had provided for the church through faithful givers. Remember, the manna continued until the very day the children of Israel began to eat the produce of the Promised Land. The Scriptures are replete with stories of God's providence.

Recapping the Chapter

First, do not be intimidated or unduly influenced by affluent people in your congregation. Do not "wine and dine" them to the exclusion of the "common folk" you serve. Smaller contributions are just as needful as one or two large ones. You do not need to be a Captain Ahab preoccupied with the obsession of harpooning a *Moby Dick*. You must be a "fisher of men," seeking the support of the multitude.

Second, work with your hands in a "tent ministry" if necessary to meet the financial needs of your family while building your congregation. This is preferable to becoming the pawn of a wealthy benefactor whose motive is to control you.

Third, do not rule out the divine provision of a loving heavenly Father who provides for His faithful ministers. Ask Elijah about the brook Cherith and the widow's meal barrel. Ask the psalmist who said, "I have never seen the righteous forsaken or their children begging bread" (Psalm 37:25, *NIV*).

Do not accept expensive personal gifts from individual members of your congregation. Many times such gifts have a large hook embedded, well hidden from view until you feel it puncture your jaw.

Also, be very cautious about accepting donated land from a family or individual on which to build a church. It is better to pay fair-market value—even to the would-be donors—than to be controlled by these donors and their descendants for generations to come.

One pastor decided to declare a moratorium on all gifts donated in the name of a loved one—living or dead. He announced a date by which any gifts such as hymnals, family Bibles, and so forth, should be reclaimed by the family. After that date all gifts in kind would become the exclusive property of the church to use or dispose of at will.

9

War Games

Pastors are leading their churches in spiritual warfare against the powers of darkness. The apostle Paul said, "For we wrestle not against flesh and blood, but against principalities, against powers, against the rulers of the darkness of this world, against spiritual wickedness in high places" (Ephesians 6:12).

Paul was obviously drawing on his knowledge of ancient Olympic games to illustrate a spiritual wrestling match to the church at Ephesus. He also admonished them, "Put on the whole armour of God, that ye may be able to stand against the wiles [trickery] of the devil" (v. 11).

Paul charged his son in the Lord, Timothy, to "fight the good fight" (1 Timothy 1:18, *NIV*). In 2 Timothy 2:3-5, Paul listed the attributes a good soldier must possess:

- He must be able to endure hardships.

- He must not entangle himself with the affairs of this world, but must seek to please the Lord.

■ He must "strive for masteries" (v. 5) and be willing to obey the rules of the games.

Even in his deathbed testimony, Paul used military language: "I have fought a good fight, I have finished my course, I have kept the faith" (2 Timothy 4:7). Ten thousand demons must have said, "Amen!"

Since the church is engaged in spiritual warfare (with much of the opposition coming from within), a brief discussion of military strategies and tactics may be appropriate.

I purposefully avoided using the words *strategies* and *tactics* until now, because they are associated with the military. The word *strategy* means "the science or art of military command as applied to the general planning and conduct of full-scale combat operations."[1] A *tactic* is "an expedient for achieving an end or the science of using strategy to gain military objectives."[2]

When young recruits are inducted into the military and sent to boot camp, part of their training involves "war games." These are realistic reconstructions and simulations of situations troops may encounter on the battlefield. Sometimes live ammunition is used for effect.

This chapter is designed to be an armchair, mini-boot camp type of experience. Hopefully, it will help young ministerial recruits prepare for battle and help the more seasoned warriors sharpen their skills.

In this chapter, selected church war games are identified by name and followed by a brief description of the strategies and tactics the local church boss may use when vying for power. This is followed by some winning strategies and tactics that have proven effective as counter measures for use in both defensive and offensive postures. Let the games begin.

Divide and Conquer

In this war game, the church boss uses his influence to divide the church into factions, making it difficult to agree. The church boss delights in trying to drive a wedge between the pastor and the congregation or members of the congregation who support the pastor and his leadership team. If he can succeed, it will be easier to devour the sheep. A shepherd separated from his flock becomes ineffective; sheep separated from the shepherd and each other become confused and easy targets for wolves.

Winning the Divide-and-Conquer Game

The antithesis of division is unity. God must be grieved by the splintering of His church. Unity is absolutely essential if the church is to fulfill the Great Commission. Jesus prayed for unity in the body of believers, and so should we. David said, "Behold how good and how pleasant it is for brethren to dwell together in unity" (Psalm 133:1).

The Holy Spirit would not have fallen on believers on the Day of Pentecost had they not been obedient in returning to Jerusalem and tarrying before the Lord in "one accord" (Acts 2:1).

If the Lord had not confounded the descendants of Noah, they would have succeeded in building the Tower of Babel, because they were united.

Even the wild beasts understand the need for unity. When a herd of musk oxen is threatened by a predator, the oxen will form a tight circle with their rumps inward and their heads turned outward. This presents a united front to the attacker. As long as the circle stays well formed with no gaps, the predator has little chance of success.[3]

To win this divisive game the pastor must be better at unifying the body than the church boss is at dividing it. An officer who wants his men to maintain their positions in the face of an attacking army must go up and down the line, often exposing himself to hostile fire. He must speak comforting and encouraging words to his troops. When the enemy realizes he cannot break through the line, he will often retreat in humiliating defeat.

A church without a vision or unity is easy to divide. A church with a vision and unity, who strive together to fulfill its vision, is almost impossible to divide.

Trench Warfare or Bulldog

This is a favorite tactic of the local church boss—dig in and hold his ground. Even when the church boss does not represent a majority opinion, he and a few determined fighters can detain progress for long periods of time—sometimes for years.

Winning the Trench Warfare Game

The best strategy against small pockets of resistance is the "pincer movement." Do not allow a handful of antagonists to impede the progress of the church. Surround them—effectively cutting them off from support groups—and move past them to implement the overall goals of the congregation. The Allies effectively used this strategy at Monte Cassino in Italy and Berlin. The

Germans used it against the Allies in the Argonne Forest "Battle of the Bulge."[4]

The Superior Numbers Game

Nathan B. Forrest, a Civil War general, was quoted as saying the way to win is to "get there first with the most men."[5] He had observed that the army arriving first on the battlefield, with the most men, had the best defensive positions. This strategy was proven effective for the confederates at Fredericksburg and for the Union Army at Gettysburg.[6]

Winning With Superior Numbers

The pastor must anticipate the moves of his opponent, beat him to the punch, and have more supporters. In other words, the pastor must be able to influence more people than his opposition.

The pastor must also learn to be a "people person." While politicians may survive on a thin margin of public approval, they seldom advance their political agendas without the approval of the majority of their constituents.

Pastors may not wish to think of themselves as *political* since that word has a bad connotation, but there is a crucial difference. When pastors shake hands and kiss babies, they sincerely care about the people they are attempting to influence.

Mercenary Soldiers

Church bosses like to use mercenaries while they themselves keep a behind-the-scenes low profile. This helps them maintain a "Mr. Good Guy" image while influencing others to do their dirty work.

Mercenaries are soldiers who work for pay. Church mercenaries work for favors or approval from the church boss. The British used German mercenary soldiers effectively against Washington's colonial troops in the Battle of Boston. But this tactic backfired at the Battle of Trenton on Christmas Day when Washington crossed the Delaware and caught the Hessian troops completely off guard.[7]

The pastor must realize mercenaries cannot contend with intense conflict. Jesus said the true shepherd will stay and protect the sheep from impending danger, but the hireling will run away at the first sign of trouble (John 10:12, 13). So it is with church bosses who beguile others into advancing their agendas.

The mercenary is willing to engage in battle only if he does not encounter resistance. When the pastor resists the mercenary's efforts to disrupt the legitimate goals of the congregation, the mercenary will flee. As he runs away, the mercenary often reveals who the actual antagonist is. The pastor usually is already aware of the identity of the person behind the mischief, but sometimes he is surprised.

The Assassination of High-Ranking Officers

Another covert tactic that church bosses use against church leaders is character assassination. Note that the word *assassinate* actually has the word *sin* embedded in it.

From a military standpoint, the assassination of high-ranking officers has always been effective. Assassination not only takes out the "brains" of the operation, but it also demoralizes the troops.

Winning Against Character Assassination

Jesus said, "Blessed are ye, when men shall revile you, and persecute you, and shall say all manner of evil against you falsely, for my sake. Rejoice, and be exceeding glad: for great is your reward in heaven: for so persecuted they the prophets which were before you" (Matthew 5:11, 12). Embedded in the poison is the antidote. When reviled and persecuted, rejoice and be glad! It will throw your accuser into a tailspin. Also, be sure the accusations are false, or the blessings housed in the scripture above cannot be claimed.

Pastors are especially vulnerable in the areas of their personal finances and their behavior with the opposite sex. As pastor, be careful to install a checks-and-balances system regarding church finances. Regarding personal finances, keep all bills current and conduct your business affairs in such a manner that you will not bring a reproach on you or your church.

When dealing with the opposite sex, especially in counseling situations, always use common sense. For example, leave the office door ajar and be sure another office worker or staff member is nearby. Keep a professional distance mentally and physically from the counselee. Also, know when and where to refer the counselee should the encounter become too personal.

It is impossible to anticipate every accusation revilers may throw at you. Jesus said they would say "all manner of evil against you" (Matthew 5:11). The best defense is to live a blameless life so their accusations will always be false. Then the accusations will have no more effect on you than a barking dog behind a tall fence. The activity is aggravating, but it cannot harm you.

Diversionary Tactics

It is a common practice in warfare to create a diversion to keep the enemy from guessing the main objective. The Allies effectively used this tactic against the Axis powers just before D-Day in Normandy.[8]

Church bosses often will use diversionary tactics against church leaders. They delight in creating distracting, disrupting events that drain the effectiveness and energy of the pastor and staff. Their main objective is to maintain control. The Scripture refers to this tactic as "sowing discord among the brethren" and is listed as one of seven things the Lord hates (see Proverbs 6:16-19).

Winning Against Diversionary Tactics

When the pastor suspects this tactic is being used, he must ask the Lord to help him stay focused. Bird hunters will tell you that when a covey of birds suddenly reveal themselves and fly in front of you, do not try to bag all the birds at once. Instead, pick out one bird and focus on it. Raise your weapon quickly and squeeze the trigger. When that bird is downed, focus on another.

In other words, do not allow the church boss to confuse and distract you with several little problems while he solidifies his control. When confronted with several problems at the same time, try to prioritize them as quickly as possible. Focus on the main problem first, solving it as quickly and judicially as possible, before moving to the next problem. This keeps you in control and denies the church boss the pleasure of seeing you run around putting out multiple fires and jumping through hoops.

The "Don't Ask, Don't Tell" Game

This game is played when a member's friend, neighbor or loved one is hospitalized and the local church office is not notified. This gives the church boss and/or irate member an opportunity to later accuse the pastor and staff of neglect.

Winning Against the "Don't Ask, Don't Tell" Game

First, it should be pointed out that visiting the sick, afflicted and incarcerated is not just the duty and responsibility of the pastor and paid staff. Every member of the body of Christ has a responsibility in this area (see Matthew 25:34-40).

Second, the pastor and his staff are not clairvoyant. If someone does not notify the church office regarding a friend or loved one in the hospital, the pastor and his staff have no way of knowing this information short of divine revelation.

Third, members should be trained to write down their prayer and visitation requests on provided booklets or cards. Busy pastors seldom remember verbalized requests beyond the current church service. Also, the pastor should keep a notepad in his suit pocket for those elbow-grabbing requests.

Recapping the Chapter

We are engaged in spiritual warfare. One way to prepare for battle is to review the strategies and tactics the enemy may use, and plan to counter his strategies and tactics.

Modern military strategists use realistic war games and simulations of actual battlefield conditions for training their troops. This chapter has attempted to review selected military strategies and tactics and then identify their spiritual equivalents to assist the pastor in "warring a good warfare."

10

Survival
Tactics

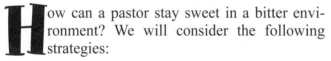

How can a pastor stay sweet in a bitter environment? We will consider the following strategies:

■ Prayer

■ Fasting and finding spiritual strength

■ Finding a confidant outside your denomination

■ Keeping a sense of humor

■ Staying physically fit

■ Finding a balance between work and play

■ Understanding your identity and who you are in Christ

When we examine the "whole armor of God," described by Paul in Ephesians 6:11-18, we discover that some tools of war, such as the "sword of the Spirit," are designed for aggression and pressing the fight to the Enemy.

Other parts of the armor serve the warrior in a defensive role such as "the helmet of salvation" (v. 17), "the breastplate of righteousness" (v. 14), and above all, "the shield of faith" (v. 16). There are times the onslaught of the Enemy is so overwhelming that all we can do is stand our ground and fight a defensive battle.

Faith is a wonderful weapon for contending "against principalities, against powers, against rulers of the darkness of this world, against spiritual wickedness in high places" (v. 12); yet the shield of faith is a defensive weapon. It is not designed to cast fear ("the sword of the Spirit, which is the Word of God," does that). The shield is there to help you survive the aggressive attack of the Enemy. Perhaps this is what Paul had in mind when he said the shield of faith would quench the fiery darts of the Enemy (v. 16).

The Romans knew how to use their shields defensively. They used a position called "the turtle" when they were under attack by archers. The soldiers on the outer perimeter of the battle group would hold their shields side-by-side forming a complete wall, while those in the middle held their shields over their heads, protecting themselves and others from flying arrows.[1]

Soldiers expect attacks from without. They stay mentally and emotionally alert, prepared to defend themselves. But what happens when the attacks catch them off guard and come from within?

While the shepherd's eyes are constantly scanning the horizon for the wolf, he is often surprised when attacked from within and behind, where the shield of faith is not as effective as a defensive weapon. In fact, the armor described in Ephesians has no protection for the back.

What can the pastor do when he is attacked from within and behind? The following survival tactics have been proven effective both in modern and Biblical times.

Prayer for the Abusive User and Persecutor

Jesus said to "pray for them which despitefully use you, and persecute you" (Matthew 5:44).

"But Jesus, surely You do not mean that I should pray for members of my congregation who have spread malicious lies about me and my family?" Yes, especially pray for them—not for their demise or destruction but for their health and well-being.

I challenge pastors to pray daily for that church boss and his family who are driving them to distraction. Do not worry about or pray for the judgment of God on them; instead, pray for their well-being. Judgment will come in time if they refuse God's mercy and patience. That matter is out of your hands.

There is Biblical precedent for praying for those who have attacked, deceived or disappointed you unjustly. Samuel continued to pray for Saul long after Israel's first king had forsaken the ways of the Lord. In fact, God had to finally tell Samuel to stop praying for Saul, because the kingdom had been given to another more worthy (see 1 Samuel 16:1).

Paul prayed for some of his companions who deserted him in a crisis and asked the Lord not to hold it against them (2 Timothy 4:16). Both Jesus (Luke 23:34) and Stephen (Acts 7:60) prayed for the very people who contributed to their deaths.

When should you pray for your antagonists? Most certainly you should pray for them during your daily devotions; but in addition, pray for them any time they cross your mind (which will be often, if they are doing their jobs effectively).

One pastor prayed for his disrupter every morning in the shower, as he was getting ready to go to the office. For the first 30 days the pastor's negative attitude toward this person did not change, but as this morning ritual continued, the pastor noticed a change. His negative thoughts became more positive toward the object of his prayers. Finally, he actually felt charitable as he prayed for the well-being of the person who had wounded him. Prayer works. It is impossible to pray for your enemies and feel animosity toward them at the same time.

Fasting and Prayer

If you really want to add power to your prayers, add the element of fasting. Developing a lifestyle of fasting and prayer should be a prerequisite for beginning one's public ministry—it was for Jesus.

Fasting has become almost unheard of in modern times, but it is a powerful spiritual weapon. The Old Testament prophets used it with great impact when they were desperate for a revelation from God. Moses fasted 40 days on Mount Sinai and again after he broke the first set of tablets.

Esther fasted and called the Jewish nation to prayer and fasting before she presented herself to the king. The result was a reversal of the king's order, which allowed the Jews to defend themselves against destruction.

When Jesus accused the Pharisees of insincere worship and public displays of adoration with their fasting and prayer, He never told them *not* to fast and pray. He told them to do these things privately before God. The apostle Paul reported being "in fastings often" (2 Corinthians 11:27). One pastor, weary of conflicts with the church boss, decided to try fasting and prayer. He set as his first goal a 21-day fast to get his own spiritual house in order. For the next three weeks he ate no solid food, drinking only water and fruit and vegetable juices to keep his fluid level up. He also took a vitamin daily for his health.

At the end of the 21 days of self-examination, the pastor had lost about 21 pounds and felt better physically and spiritually than he had in a long time. He realized that a longer fast on behalf of the local church was attainable. He felt the urging of the Holy Spirit to plan a 40-day fast in conjunction with a six-week period of revival at the local church sponsored by his denomination.

Again he ate no solid food except a few olives each evening, washing them down with tomato juice to maintain a healthy PH balance.

The schedule for the next six weeks was rigorous. Every weekend there was a special event or speaker connected with the revival. The pastor discovered that if he paced himself with brief periods of rest during the day, he was able to not only maintain his normal schedule, but also keep up with the revival events.

Some of the members, seeing their pastor's demonstration of love and devotion to the congregation, held him up with periods of fasting and prayer of their own. Church attendance did not dramatically increase, but

Games Local Church Bosses Play

some new families started attending. Those who had been critical of the pastor lost their credibility, and a godly fear settled over the congregation.

The pastor kept a daily log of his activities and revelations during this time, which are too numerous to share in this book. He saw no angels nor did God speak to him in an audible voice; but he did receive three distinct impressions from God that strengthened him for the remainder of his tenure as pastor of that local congregation.

On day 13 of the fast, the Spirit impressed him that He was going to begin a healing process for that congregation from the bones outward. This impression was so strong and strange the pastor searched for a Biblical precedent. The nearest reference he could find was the account of Ezekiel and the valley of dry bones (see Ezekiel 37).

The second impression occurred on day 14 of the fast. The Spirit spoke to the pastor's heart, saying, "When there is an abundance of bread in the land, the people do not pray."

The next impression occurred in a dream. The Spirit told the pastor that He was placing a moat of protection around him. His antagonists might come to the edge of the moat and try to distract him, but they would be unable to inflict any harm.

The church enjoyed a period of rest after this time of fasting and prayer. This was brought about in no small measure by the demise of two of the pastor's detractors. One asked the pastor's forgiveness shortly before his death. The other one never did seek reconciliation and went to meet his Maker thinking he had done God and the congregation a favor by appointing himself the "keeper of the faith."

102

I would like to report a happy ending to this story. I would like to say that both the pastor and the congregation enjoyed many years of growth and spiritual renewal, but it did not happen that way. The pastor battled with the church boss, but although his last year was rather pleasant and rewarding, his effectiveness was gone. He elected to move on to another challenge.

What church bosses fail to understand is when the pastor's energy and creativity are drained from constant badgering, he has little energy left to build the kingdom of God. One day church bosses will be held accountable for that.

Find a Friend and Confidant Outside Your Denomination

Where does the pastor go when he needs a friend with whom to share his dreams and frustrations? He cannot talk to members of the congregation about his frustrations, lest he be viewed as a whiner. He cannot tell everything to his wife, lest he make her feel insecure because of his anxieties.

In addition, he cannot discuss his frustrations with colleagues, because every denomination has a grapevine. Soon his personal and private life would be a hot topic of discussion as telephones jingle and e-mails surge across the continent faster than a speeding bullet.

An alternative is to find a fellow pastor from another denomination with whom you can bare your soul without concern that someone from your congregation may hear about it. An added bonus is that you serve as a neutral sounding board for your fellow pastor as well. He can bare his soul to you.

How do you meet pastors from other denominations? One way is to become an active participant in your local ministerial association. Not only will you be blessed by the ecumenical involvement, but you will almost always meet one or two fellow pastors with whom you will develop a close friendship.

One pastor reported that he and his cross-denominational friend had a scheduled breakfast together once a week to share ideas and frustrations. This was a defusing session in a casual and safe environment. They also kept their ministries sharp by discussing what they had been reading lately. They also talked of doctrinal differences in a nonthreatening manner. It was therapeutic and intellectually stimulating for both pastors.

Keeping a Sense of Humor

While it is difficult to maintain a sense of humor during the time you are being hammered by the church boss, it is necessary to keep things in perspective and save your sanity.

The Scripture says, "A merry heart [laughter] doeth good like a medicine" (Proverbs 17:22). In the worst of times, you must be able to laugh at yourself and your situation.

Jesus said, "Blessed are ye, when men shall revile you, and persecute you, and shall say all manner of evil against you falsely, for my sake. Rejoice and be exceeding glad" (Matthew 5:11, 12). Why would Jesus tell us to rejoice and be very glad at such times? He knew it would be good for us mentally, emotionally and spiritually.

One pastor said a church boss once implied he could not "preach his way out of a wet paper bag." The visual image of actually coming to the pulpit draped in a huge wet bag and trying to preach his way out of it struck him so humorously, it actually inspired him for the next several Sundays. He seriously considered trying the wet bag bit just to see if he could do it.

Then there is the timely and witty comeback. When one church boss told his pastor, "All preachers are compulsive liars," the pastor replied, "It's a good thing we are, because some day one of us will have to conduct your funeral."

Folklore from the Vietnam War includes a story regarding a detachment of marines who were surrounded and cut off from reinforcements by an overwhelming number of Vietcong. The battle was fierce and sometimes hand-to-hand. Wave after wave of the North Vietnam forces were driven back only to charge again with renewed energy and determination.

When the marines realized they might not survive the next attack, they decided to die laughing. When the next wave of Vietcong hit their line, they all broke into loud laughter. It so demoralized the enemy that they retreated in confusion and did not launch another attack! Captured members of the Vietcong unit were still relating this story months later to their captors.

Pastor, if you can learn the art of self-deprecating humor, it will help you walk through murky waters and dark valleys. You should be warned, however, that pastors' wives do not always appreciate their husbands' pulpit humor—especially if it is self-deprecating. Only the user understands the need for it. When life is not funny, laugh anyway.

Staying Physically Fit

Boot camp is designed to recruit a group of "couch potatoes" and in a few weeks shape them into fighting machines. They are trained to march 20 miles with a 70-pound field pack, fight a major battle, and then do it all over again with very little rest.

A pastor's schedule is not as vigorous as boot camp, but there will be days and weeks you will feel like it is. It is absolutely essential that you stay physically fit. The apostle Paul's many references to the Olympic Games leads us to believe that the apostle was well acquainted with the need for physical fitness.

Encouraging pastors to eat right, exercise, and get enough rest sounds almost too basic, but it is true nonetheless. If you do not take care of your body, who will? The congregation you are working yourself literally to death for will not appreciate that fact when you are gone. And even if they do, it will not bring you back to your pulpit or your family. If you are a self-starter you can do this on your own. If not, join a health club.

Find a Balance Between Work and Play

From time to time, Jesus called His disciples to a period of rest and relaxation. On one occasion, they were being mobbed by the crowds and did not even have time to eat.

If Jesus and His disciples needed rest and relaxation, so do you. Find a hobby or pastime radically different from your normal ministerial duties and engage in it as often as your schedule will allow. Some find distraction on the golf course, while others love the thrill of casting a fly rod in a remote mountain stream. There are thousands of other options—find one.

One reason most pastors fail to find a balance between productive work and therapeutic play is a false sense of guilt when they are temporarily away from their ministerial duties and responsibilities. Remember, you also have a responsibility to yourself and your family. Taking time to relax and engage in therapeutic play refreshes you with new vigor.

Understanding Your Identity

In one of the darkest hours in the life of the apostle Paul, an angel from God appeared to him and assured him everything would be all right. When he reported this message of hope to his fellow shipmates, he used the possessive pronoun phrase "whose I am" to describe his relationship to God (Acts 27:23).

Sometimes in your darkest hour, you have to remember "whose" you are. You are not just a child of God—you are a chosen vessel to carry the gospel of the Lord Jesus Christ, a clay pot in which God has deposited His most valuable and important gift.

Try this exercise when you are really feeling down. It sounds elementary and a little silly, but it is effective. Stand in front of a mirror, look yourself right in the eyes, and repeat the question "Whose am I?" several times to yourself. Stand there until the answer comes to you. The battle is not yours—it's God's.

You are important to God. You are His eyes, ears, hands and feet in this dark world. He cannot afford to let you fail.

When the Lord Jesus appeared in all His power and glory to the apostle John in Revelation, He addressed His admonitions to the "angels of the seven churches" of Asia (see Revelation 2; 3). Most Bible scholars seem to agree the word *angel* here refers to the pastors of the seven churches.[2]

Think of it. The Lord himself thinks of you as an angel if you are pastoring one of His flocks. By the way, all seven of the churches were wrestling with one or more serious problems. If you are searching for a church with no problems, you will not find one.

Recapping the Chapter

Do not underestimate the power of praying for the health and well-being of those who despitefully use you. When prayer is combined with the ancient ritual of fasting, it forms a powerful wall of defense.

Second, you must keep a sense of humor in the face of adversity. Those who laugh at themselves and their circumstances survive longer than those who find no humor in life.

Third, finding a confidant outside your own denomination is both healthy and rewarding. To be able to talk freely to someone outside of your denomination is comforting and nonthreatening.

Fourth, no soldier should go to war without being physically fit, and neither should you. Eat right, engage in some form of physical exercise, and try to get sufficient rest. Your body will thank you and so will your family.

Fifth, find a balance between productive work and therapeutic play. Jesus found it necessary to come away and rest awhile (Mark 6:31) with His disciples. Remember, He could have called on His divine energy to keep going, but He was setting an example for the disciples.

Finally, know "whose" you are. You are God's anointed "angel" filled with the gospel of grace, commissioned to carry the message of life to a dark and dying sea of humanity who desperately needs to hear what you have to say.

11

Collusion
With the
Staff

One of the favorite tactics that church bosses use on pastors is to find one or more staff members who lean toward disloyalty to the pastor and exploit the situation. This chapter will assist pastors in maintaining the loyalty of staff members. For example, when searching for a staff member to fill a particular need, the pastor should look for someone who is a specialist in that area and has no ambition for a pulpit ministry. That is presumably why the church hired the senior pastor. Otherwise, he may enter his office one day and find an ambitious staff member sitting at the desk mentally measuring for curtains and looking for space on the wall to hang his diplomas. This chapter is not designed to make the pastor paranoid, but it suggests using caution and wisdom.

Choosing Staff Members

Selecting staff members that work in harmony with

each other to advance the agenda of the local church is a tedious and important process. Some larger multistaff congregations promote from within and have a step-by-step program for aspiring staff members. Those members of the congregation who wish to become permanent full-time staff members must be willing to accept the most menial of tasks—such as custodial duties—to be considered for a full-time position. The idea is to prove them faithful in small matters before being given responsibility in larger matters.

Other congregations hire specialists for staffing positions. For example, if they are looking for a youth pastor, they look for someone who is a "career" youth pastor and has no desire or ambition to serve as senior pastor. This eliminates the "preacher's itch" suffered by some aspiring staffers who are just using their current position as a stepping-stone to the senior pastor position. The exceptions would be interns and heirs apparent.

Regardless of the methods used to select staff members, the one trait they must possess is loyalty to the senior pastor. If this does not exist, the alert church boss will detect it and exploit the situation. Satan fell from grace when he got his eye on the big chair. Many staff members have been tempted to ally with the church bosses to unseat the senior pastor.

How does the senior pastor guard against such collusion without becoming paranoid, while building a productive and harmonious working relationship with staff members? The key word is *relationship*. Whether we are talking about a small church with one part-time secretary or a large congregation with multimember staff, the senior pastor must build healthy working relationships with his staff members.

There was a time in Western society when a man's word was his bond and business agreements were confirmed with a handshake. Such is not the case today, even among churches. A written covenant or agreement is usually drawn up and signed by all parties concerned to attempt to ensure that mutual expectations will be carried out.

One church outlined its staff expectations in an employee manual titled "Mutual Expectations Covenant." The senior pastor and all paid staff members signed the agreement. The agreement detailed the mutual expectations of the senior pastor, staff members and the congregation.

While behavior cannot be legislated, it helps to have certain things in black and white to minimize confusion and prevent misunderstandings. It also provides a basis for performance evaluation. A written agreement makes it more difficult for a local church boss to drive a wedge between a staff member and the senior pastor.

However, a written document is no better than the people who sign it. In the final analysis, both the senior pastor and the staff members must be willing to work toward achieving a harmonious working relationship. Some mutual expectations between the senior pastor and staff members are listed below.

What the Senior Pastor Should Expect From Staff Members

Loyalty. A pastor must have the absolute loyalty of each member of his staff. A loyal staff member would never undermine the pastor or his programs.

Trust. A pastor should expect staff members to be trustworthy. A staff member's word should be his/her bond.

Faithfulness. A pastor should expect a staff member to be faithful to the fulfillment of his/her duties and responsibilities.

Dedication. The pastor should expect a staff member to have a high level of dedication to assigned tasks and be self-motivated.

Promptness. The pastor should expect staff members to be prompt in attendance to all church services, special events and work schedules. Habitual tardiness is not an acceptable personality trait for staff members. Also, assigned tasks should be completed in a timely manner.

Support. Every senior pastor develops an agenda of programs for the local church. Staff members are expected to undergird these programs with their creative energy and prayerful support.

Godliness. The pastor should expect staff members to live morally correct lives consistent with Biblical principles.

Honesty/integrity. The manner in which staff members conduct their personal business affairs is of vital importance to the church and pastor. The pastor expects staff members to pay their bills in a timely manner and conduct all business dealings with a high level of integrity that will not bring a reproach on the church.

Positive attitude. Success in all fields of endeavor including the church depends on maintaining a positive attitude and outlook. The pastor expects staff members to talk and act positively regarding all aspects of the church. This does not mean that the pastor wants to surround himself with "yes-men."

Respect and love. The position of pastor is that of anointed leader. Both the office and the person may expect love and respect from staff members.

Prayer. The pastor should expect staff members and their families to hold him and his family up to God in prayer.

Model family leadership. Since so much of church life is built around family life (and vice versa), it is imperative that staff members be models of Christian values in the home. Spouse or child abuse in any form (physical, mental/emotional or sexual) will not be tolerated. The pastor should expect staff members to exhibit Biblical principles in interpersonal family relationships. A person who does not have his own house in order should not serve in a leadership capacity in the church (1 Timothy 3:1-5).

Team effort. The pastor should expect staff members to function as a team. This means maximizing individual skills and abilities while balancing individual plans and programs for the good of the whole. Interdepartmental jealousy and undermining is not conducive to team effort (Luke 9:46-48).

Appropriate dress. The senior pastor should expects staff members to dress appropriately. Thought should be given to modesty and the maintaining of a professional image. This is especially important when ministering in the sanctuary.

Accountability. Someone has said, "It is not just what is expected, but what is inspected that gets done." Accountability is a vital link in the pastor/staff member relationship. Whether this comes in the form of periodic written reports, annual formal personnel evaluations, or informal visits by the pastor to various areas of ministry, accountability is an important and reasonable expectation.

What Staff Members Should Expect From the Senior Pastor

Members of the pastor's staff constitute an inner circle of believers. The senior pastor has a special obligation to serve in the role of pastor to these individuals and their immediate families. In this role, the pastor holds them up in prayer, visits them when they are sick, and counsels with them when they just need someone who will listen.

Appreciation. Like most people, staff members work better when they feel appreciated for the work they do. The wise senior pastor will express appreciation in word and deed both publicly and privately. This is a reasonable expectation that pays high dividends.

Support. Staff members should expect the senior pastor to be supportive of the programs in their respective departments. If things are organized (as they should be), these programs compliment the master plan of the church and work hand in hand with the senior pastor's goals and objectives. Support comes in many forms and includes budgeting, recruiting workers and occasional attendance at selected events.

Defense from attack. From time to time, a staff member may come under unwarranted attack or criticism from a well-meaning church member, church elder or member of the community. At such times it is imperative for the pastor to make every reasonable effort to gather the facts in the case and then stand by the staff member as the situation demands.

The articulation of short- and long-term goals and objectives. Staff members should expect the senior pastor to articulate his vision for the church in the form of short- and long-term goals and objectives. This is a valuable aid in departmental planning; it also assures that departmental goals and objectives will compliment the master plan for the church.

Word-centered ministry. Staff members should expect the senior pastor to preach and teach from a Word-centered perspective. This provides a role model for all staff members, department heads and teachers (2 Timothy 4:2).

Positive relationships. The senior pastor walks a fine line between being a friend to the staff members and being their immediate supervisor. This dual role sometimes creates conflict, but it also provides opportunities for relationship building, which is so vital to team effort. Relationship building works best when all parties have a positive attitude toward it and tenures of office are lengthy enough to build it. Staff members should normally expect to have a positive relationship with the senior pastor and vice versa.

Godliness. Staff members look to the senior pastor as a role model of godly living consistent with Biblical principles of moral conduct. He should also be an example in his personal and corporate prayer life and devotion to the Word. This is a reasonable expectation for a spiritual leader (1 Timothy 3:1-7).

Desire to fulfill the Great Commission. There should be a mutual expectation between pastor and staff members that everyone involved in the work of the Kingdom will have the fulfillment of the Great Commission as his/her number one priority (Mark 16:15, 16).[1]

Pastor/Staff Retreats

One of the ways the senior pastor and the staff can build relationships is the pastor/staff retreat. One or two times per year the pastor and his staff need to get away from the office and busy schedules to relax in a casual environment. Retreats can involve productive work and therapeutic play.

Retreats can have a central theme (such as developing the church calendar for the upcoming year) or they may have an open agenda where departmental concerns and conflicts can be ironed out.

If the church does not have a written mission statement, the pastor/staff retreat is a good place to develop one. This presumes, of course, that a wide spectrum of input has already been obtained from the congregation.

The most important thing that takes place on a retreat is the building of relationships. Both the pastor and the staff need to see each other outside the formal environment of the church. To involve spouses and children, at least in the therapeutic play portion of the retreat, is a bonus.

Management Styles

Much has been said in the corporate world regarding management styles. Since most staff members answer directly to the senior pastor, it's important to have a good match between the pastor's management style and work ethic, and the staff members.

Some pastors are rather laid back in their management styles, allowing staffers to determine their own departmental goals and work schedules. Other pastors are time-and-task driven and feel a need to micromanage the departmental goals and work schedules of staff members. Some pastors choose to lead by example. While setting high expectations for themselves, they do not force staff members to comply—only to observe and follow.

Whatever the management style of the senior pastor, it is important that selected staff members are compatible. Disgruntled staff members become easy targets and soul mates for disgruntled church members who may drive the pastor to distraction.

The Absalom Syndrome

Every Sunday school student is familiar with the story of Absalom, one of King David's handsome young sons, who led a rebellion against his father. Absalom had already shown himself capable of capital murder when he plotted and carried out the murder of his half brother, Amnon, for raping his sister Tamar (2 Samuel 13:22-29).

Rather than execute his son for this vile deed, David exiled him from court for an extended period of time. When he was allowed to return home, he was not immediately welcomed back at court. Even when he was received and forgiven, a certain closeness he had enjoyed with his father was forever broken.

A plot began to take root in Absalom's mind. Why couldn't he take his father's throne? His method of rebellion, at first, was covert. After all, he was handsome and popular with the people. Why not stand at the entrance to the king's court and receive aggrieved citizens with a warm handshake and a promise to help solve their problems? He was the adroit politician willing to promise the moon in exchange for the goodwill of the people—and it worked.

Over a period of time, Absalom won the hearts of the people from his aging father, David. Now came step two in his plan. His methods changed. He convinced key people to follow him. He raised an army, proclaimed himself king, and led an armed rebellion against his father that almost succeeded.

Why have we taken the time to recite this old Sunday school story? Because if you change the characters a little bit and move the story to modern times, you have the makings of a church rebellion. Let the senior pastor be King David and a popular staff member or associate pastor play Absalom's role. You can readily see how a church split can come about with the alliance of a disgruntled staff member and a local church boss.

What caused Absalom to turn against his own father and lead a rebellion against him? Their fellowship and, therefore, their relationship had been broken. In order to keep the "Absalom syndrome" from infecting staff members, the senior pastor must do all he can to maintain fellowship and healthy relationships with staff members. However, the total responsibility does not fall only on the senior pastor. Staff members have an obligation to resist becoming infected with the Absalom syndrome.

If a staff member becomes infected with this fatal disease in spite of everything the pastor, staff and church governing body can do, the infected staffer should be asked to resign or be terminated. Remember, Absalom ended up hanging by his hair from the branches of a tree with multiple wounds in his chest inflicted by David's loyal soldiers.

Recapping the Chapter

Good staffing begins with careful selection. If your church has a policy of promoting from within, aspiring full-time staff members should be given part-time positions first to test their faithfulness. They must first demonstrate faithfulness over a few things before you make them "ruler" of many things.

Hire specialists who are career ministers in their chosen field. This will eliminate the temptation for staffers to use their current position as a stepping-stone to "greater" things—like perhaps your job.

To avoid the infectious "Absalom syndrome," where a popular staffer undermines the senior pastor with the congregation, a healthy relationship must be developed and maintained between the senior pastor and the staff. While good relationships cannot be legislated nor mandated, there are some steps that can be taken to enhance relationships.

Good relationships flow out of good communication. Verbal commendations for a job well done go a long way in building relationships between the senior pastor and his staff. Also, a written covenant of mutual expectations helps to clarify areas of duties and responsibilities. Finally, staff retreats build relationships and provide a time for planning.

Absolute loyalty is the primary attribute that a senior pastor should expect from a staff member. Anything less leads to poor relationships and opens the door for a local church boss to take advantage of the situation. This game is called "divide and conquer."

12

The Danger of Touching God's Anointed

The Scriptures are replete with examples of the tragic results of what happens when people touch or harm God's anointed leaders by word or deed. This chapter will not only examine selected Biblical accounts, but it will also share a true modern-day Ananias and Sapphira story with the tragic results.

The goal is to raise the awareness of pastors and would-be church bosses to the very real dangers in harming God's anointed leaders. It is a dangerous thing to trifle with a man of God; yet local church bosses do it with impunity, not considering the dire consequences of their behavior.

The Story of David and Saul

David wisely chose not to harm King Saul because he was the anointed leader of God's people. Even long after Saul had forsaken the ways of the Lord, David would not lift his hand against him.

David had many opportunities to kill Saul and would have been justified in doing so. First, Saul was pursuing David maliciously, intending to murder him without just cause. If David had killed him, it would have been self-defense.

Second, David himself had already been anointed by the prophet Samuel to take Saul's place. Eliminating Saul would have set the stage for David to take his rightful place on the throne of Israel.

Still David would not lift his hand against Saul because Saul was the Lord's anointed leader. David could have killed him in the cave or he could have killed him in the field while he slept.

Even when Saul met his tragic end on Mount Gilboa, David did not rejoice. Instead he mourned his death. When the young man who brought the news of Saul's death to David expected a reward, he was put to the sword for having the audacity to harm God's anointed leader (see 2 Samuel 1:1-16).

The Story of Samson

In the end, the Philistines paid a heavy price for hiring Delilah to seduce Samson. They shaved his locks and ruined his eyes with no regard that he was a man of God. What his enemies forgot is that hair grows back. The anointing returned at the time of his death, and Samson slew more Philistines than he had slain in his life.

The Criticizing Sister

Miriam, the sister of Moses, was smitten with leprosy from head to toe for criticizing her brother for his choice of a wife. If her brother had not entreated God on her behalf, Miriam would have died a miserable death.

Others who murmured against Moses were killed by poisonous snakebites or swallowed up by the earth. Even his own nephews, Nadab and Abihu, were slain at the entrance of the tabernacle when they presumed to offer strange fire before the Lord in rebellion against their uncle.

New Testament Incidents

In the New Testament, Ananias and his wife, Sapphira, fell dead when they lied to the Holy Spirit by misrepresenting the amount of their offering to God's anointed leader.

In a modern version of the Ananias and Sapphira story, one congregation reported that a member fell dead in the lobby of the church while he was attempting to lead a rebellious walkout on the pastor.

Another pastor said while he was preparing a message on rebellion, his phone rang and a frantic voice asked him to come quickly. One of his senior members, who had been active in his opposition to the pastor, had just suffered a heart attack and stroke. He lingered in a comatose state for a few days but passed on without ever regaining consciousness.

In Acts 20:29, 30, the apostle Paul relates having to deal with false brethren. And when he gathered the elders from the church at Ephesus at the boat dock for prayers, he warned them that after his departure "grievous wolves" would slip in among them, not sparing the flock (v. 29). Even some of the elders themselves would rebel against the church and lead some members off into heresy.

I have often wondered what ever happened to the man who slapped Paul in the face when he was testifying before the high priest. Or what the outcome was for those Jews who placed themselves under a curse and refused to eat until Paul was dead by their hand. Since Paul survived at least another three years, they would have either perished from self-imposed starvation or broken their vow and incurred the curse. More than 40 men were involved in this conspiracy.

Christian tradition says the daughter of Herodias, the dancer who asked for the head of John the Baptist on a platter, died a tragic and painful death. She touched God's anointed only as a proxy for her wicked mother, but she suffered the consequences just the same.

Time would fail us to recount (and we don't even know) all the tragic endings of those who persecuted Jesus. Pilate, according to Josephus, lost his post. Christian tradition says Pilate lost his mind and would wash his hands over and over. Judas hanged himself after betraying the Lord with a kiss.

In the popular film *The Robe*, Marcellus, the Roman centurion who supervised the crucifixion, went insane and asked the question repeatedly, "Were you out there?" Later in the film, his sanity was restored when he accepted Jesus as his Lord and Savior.

Dozens of soldiers, religious leaders and common folk assaulted Jesus that day by slapping, spitting or just yelling, "Crucify Him!" Many of these same people were still around in A.D. 70 when the Roman general Titus besieged and eventually destroyed Jerusalem. At one point Josephus reported that Titus was having as many as 500 Jews per day crucified. His soldiers reported running out of wood to make crosses and had to wait for bodies to be removed so fresh victims could be nailed to the crude instruments of torture. They had touched God's anointed, and now they were paying a horrible price. Did any of them remember they had stood before Pilate and screamed, "Let his blood be on us and on our children?" (Matthew 27:25, *NIV*).

In our own generation, the ravages of the Holocaust are well known. If our civilization stands another thousand years, those unthinkable activities carried out by Hitler and his executioners will continue to be dramatized in films, songs and plays.

Additional Incidents of Touching God's Anointed

- Cain murdered his righteous brother, Abel, out of jealousy and suffered exile from the presence of God. By his own testimony his punishment was more than he could bear (Genesis 4:13).

- Abimelech took Sarah into his household thinking she was Abraham's sister and not his wife. Fortunately, he did not have intimate relations with her before he discovered Abraham's little "white lie." Even so, God struck all the women of Abimelech's household with barrenness until Sarah was returned home and Abraham prayed for their healing (see Genesis 20).

- Pharaoh was "plagued" by God for harassing Moses and Aaron and hardening his heart against God's people. When he finally said to God's anointed leaders, "I do not wish to see your faces again," he got his wish, but he lost his firstborn son in the process, as did every Egyptian family not protected by the blood of the Passover lamb.

■ The judgment of God fell on Balaam for attempting to curse the chosen people. Remember? He was the one who carried on a conversation with a donkey (Numbers 22:21-41). This gives you some idea of the mental state of the church boss's forerunner in the Old Testament.

■ Even children and young people are not exempt from the judgment of God when they touch His anointed leaders, as we see in 2 Kings 2. As Elisha was traveling up to Samaria, some children came out from a village and began to taunt the man of God by calling him "baldhead" (v. 23). Elisha promptly pronounced a curse on them, and two bears came out of the woods and mauled 42 children. They had assaulted God's anointed with their tongues and paid the price with their bodies.

The Church Age

The apostle John makes one of the more obvious New Testament references to a local church boss in his third epistle. A man named Diotrephes fits the profile well. His very name means "an opponent of Christianity."

> I wrote unto the church: but Diotrephes, who loveth to have the preeminence among them, receiveth us not. Wherefore, if I come, I will remember his deeds which he doeth, prating against us with mali-

cious words: and not content therewith, neither doth he himself receive the brethren, and forbiddeth them that would, and casteth them out of the church (3 John 9, 10).

Long before the days of the Holiday Inn, it was common courtesy to receive traveling preachers, teachers and evangelists into homes, providing them with food and shelter while they proclaimed the gospel. The apostle John had apparently sent some travelers on their way to their next appointment with a recommendation for the saints to receive them and provide them with Christian hospitality. When the travelers came to the church where Diotrephes had appointed himself in charge, he not only refused to receive them, but he also forbade others to do so, threatening to excommunicate those who did not obey him.

This behavior infuriated John. The old "son of thunder" informed the church that he would deal with the problem when he arrived in person.

When we analyze the behavior of Diotrephes, we see certain familiar patterns. First of all, John said he "loveth to have the preeminence among them" (v. 9). The word *preeminence* in the original language meant "to be fond of being first, i.e. ambitious of distinction: love to have the preeminence."[1] In other words, Diotrephes loved to be in charge of things and evidently had grown accustomed to "bullying" the other members of the church, including the pastor. Does any of this sound familiar?

Second, John says, Diotrephes was guilty of "prating against us with malicious words" (v. 10). The word *prating* is used only three times in Scripture. Solomon used the term twice in Proverbs, and John uses it here. Proverbs says, "The wise in heart will receive commandments: but a prating fool shall fall . . . He that winketh with the eye [overlooks injustice] causeth sorrow: but a prating fool shall fall" (10:8, 10). In the Hebrew language *prating* meant "the use of vain words."[2] In the Greek New Testament it meant, "to be a babbler or trifler: to berate idly or mischievously."[3]

Of the two charges the apostle brought against Diotrephes—being a prating or babbling fool, heading for destruction, and that of loving to have the preeminence—the latter was a more serious charge. Diotrephes was trying to usurp the authority of Christ in the church. The only other place the word *preeminence* is used in the New Testament is in Colossians 1:18, which speaks directly about Christ being the head of the church or having preeminence.

When a modern-day Diotrephes or church boss tries to usurp authority, he is actually trying to push Christ himself out of His designated position as head of the church. Of course, any attempt to usurp the pastor's authority has the same effect, since the pastor serves in a shepherding role under the Chief Shepherd. Also, the Founder of the church will make it very clear at the Judgment that any neglect or abuse to His people is considered neglect or abuse of Christ himself.

The church boss who touches God's anointed leader is setting himself up for a catastrophic fall and a court date at the judgment bar.

Recapping the Chapter
Both the Old and New Testaments show the danger of

touching or harming God's anointed leader by word or deed. Why do we continue to have blatant violations of this spiritual law? We can only assume that either the violator is ignorant of the Holy Scripture, or the temptation to usurp, dominate or control is overwhelming. There is at least one other possibility—the church boss actually thinks he is doing God a favor by "keeping the pastor in line." In any case, judgment is coming and it will not be pleasant for the perpetrator.

13

Fight or Flight

There comes a time in every pastor's ministry when he has to make a decision to either stay in his current position or move on to a new challenge. This chapter will examine both sides of the issue and attempt to give the pastor some Biblical and practical considerations to help him make a good decision.

Adrenaline and Anointing

Thank God for adrenaline. It is a wonderful chemical enhancer produced by the body itself when you find yourself in a situation that requires you to stand and fight or run away. The anointing of the Holy Spirit is the spiritual equivalent to adrenaline. The Holy Spirit will either give you the strength and courage to stand and fight against evil—even when it is found in the pews of the church—or give you wisdom to know when it is time to move on to a new challenge.

The apostle Paul was sometimes called by the Spirit to minister in certain areas. At other times he was restrained or forbidden by the Spirit to minister in other areas. The Scripture does promise that "the steps of a good man are ordered by the Lord" (Psalm 37:23).

The problem is, after you have been butted about for months or years by a church boss, you may not be in the right frame of mind to make a good decision. Pull yourself together, remember "whose" you are, and ask the Holy Spirit to direct your path. You cannot always trust your feelings, so trust your faith. Remember, the Lord is going to love you whether you decide to stay or move on to a new challenge. But you owe it to yourself, your family and your church to prayerfully weigh the advantages and disadvantages of leaving your current post.

Consider the following questions when making this decision:

- Will my staying be detrimental to my family or to me mentally, emotionally or spiritually?

- Will my staying enhance the growth and spiritual health of the congregation?

- Is there anything I can say or do that would make a difference in the power structure of the church?

When you look deep inside and find honest answers to these questions, you will have come a long way toward making a correct decision to stay or go.

The Case for Going

Should you decide to relocate, do not think of yourself as one of the "hireling" shepherds that Jesus mentions in John 10. First, the hirelings Jesus referred to ran away at the first sign of danger. If you have been at your current post of duty for a reasonable period of time, you obviously did not retreat at the first sign of danger.

Second, when you answered the question at the beginning of this chapter regarding the health and well-being of your family, what was the answer? If your staying would be detrimental to your spouse or children, your first responsibility is to your family. Long before there was an organized church, there was family. If you are forced to decide between congregation and family, choose family.

There are many preacher's kids who became permanently alienated from the church after watching their parents being shoved through the meat grinder of the local church boss.

In the Old Testament, it was a simple matter to know when it was time to break camp and move. The cloud, which represented the presence of God, hovered over the Tent of Meeting until it was time to move, and then the cloud would lead them to the new location.

Today the Holy Spirit can be just as real in guiding our steps as the cloud was to the children of Israel. The apostle Paul tried to stay sensitive to the leading of the Spirit in his action-filled ministry. He stayed at Ephesus a short period of time, but he remained at the school of Tyrannus about two years.

In his letters to Timothy, Paul encouraged him to stay as pastor of the church at Ephesus. Later, Paul sent Tychicus to pastor the church and asked for Timothy to hasten to Rome to see him before winter.

It is not only possible but probable that God sent you to a particular congregation to accomplish certain predetermined things. When those things are done, it is time for you to move on to a new challenge.

Moses and Aaron were willing to stay in Egypt long enough to convince Pharaoh to let the children of Israel depart in peace. But when the time came for them to leave, they left "lock, stock and barrel," with an extra pair of traveling shoes in their hand. Even though the people sometimes wondered if they had made a good decision to leave Egypt, Moses never wavered about the correctness of the decision.

The "Hallelujah Chorus"

I shall never forget driving away from a particularly difficult pastorate. The U-Haul was packed to the brim with almost all of the family's accumulated goods. Handel's *Messiah* was in the tape player cued to the "Hallelujah Chorus." Just as the moving van crossed the city-limit sign, I pressed the button and a magnificent choir, accompanied by the Philharmonic orchestra, flooded the cab with powerful, pulsating music to free the soul. My wife was in the pace car and from a pre-arranged hand signal, we both joined our voices in celebration of leaving this particular assignment.

Yet, before the music faded, we felt a twinge of sadness for the good people we were leaving behind—those who had stood with us in the trenches against the tyrannical local church boss. Some had held us up in prayer every day for 912 days. They wept when we wept and rejoiced when we rejoiced. Some fasted with us when we went through the dark valley. We could not have survived without them, and we shall never forget their kindness. Now

Paul's letters to the churches have new meaning for us. We recognize some of our friends in the persons of the choice saints he greeted in his salutations. They were our joy.

But we were leaving battered and bruised from our close encounter with the power structure of the church. Even though they were a minority, they were loud and aggressive, drowning out the voices of the gentle saints who so desperately wanted us to stay.

We were fortunate to return to our home church—not to pastor, but to receive ministry. For a whole year, I did not step into a pulpit. We just came to church and soaked up the good fellowship with people we loved and who loved us.

At the end of the year, with reserve funds running low, it was time to get back into the ministry. Yet we were not sure we wanted back in the mainstream.

Three employment opportunities came almost at the same time. One was a secular job in my field of educational administration and supervision. The salary and benefit package was attractive. Two opportunities were in ministry. One was full-time with a lucrative package. The other was part-time, and the initial salary offering was not even sufficient to meet our basic needs. We took it anyway because it was where we felt the Lord wanted us to be.

That was four years ago at this writing, and we have no regrets. The salary and benefit package has improved over time, and best of all, God has allowed us to stay where we are loved and appreciated.

Our wounds have healed from our encounter with our "Diotrephes." He has gone on to his reward and we hope to see him again in a better place and time, when we shall all give account to the Chief Shepherd. We hold neither bitterness nor remorse. The fiery trials we endured have made us better people and greatly increased our value in the ministry.

The Case for Staying

Until recently, there seemed to be a tendency among pastors to "get out of the kitchen" when the heat got too hot. Some are now discovering that the best cooking takes place in a hot kitchen! The trend is shifting to long-term pastorates. Strong arguments can be made to support the idea of claiming a city or geographical area for God and then settling in for the long haul.

Usually, the local church boss has one decided advantage—he is not going anywhere. He and members of his family have probably occupied the pews of their church for three or four generations or more. Somewhere in a dusty trunk in his basement, he probably has the bullet-riddled Bibles of every former pastor, much like the bad guys in a cheap western keep the tin star of each previous town sheriff. If the pastor leaves, the boss wins.

It has been said that a local church does not really begin to catch the vision of a new pastor until he has been there for at least five years. It often takes this long to "win friends and influence people" and recruit members who are favorable to your vision for the church into key positions.

John Maxwell contends that since 20 percent of the people do 80 percent of the work in a church, the pastor should identify these people and spend 80 percent of his time with them. They, in turn, will help him succeed in ministry.[1]

Longevity gives the pastor and his family several advantages both at church and in the community:

- If he has school-age children, they can complete their formal education in one school system.

- The pastor has time to become well-known and respected in the community.

- The pastor does not have to start over from square one in building relationships both in the church and in the community.

- There is a sense of security and permanence in the long-term pastorate. (The pastor's wife and children especially like this one.)

- There is the remote possibility that over a period of time, a long-term pastor may even earn the love and respect of the local church boss.

John Maxwell tells the story of a newly appointed pastor who decided to confront the local church boss right up front. He called his antagonist into the church office and laid the cards on the table. He told him that his reputation as a bully of pastors was well-known. He reminded the church boss that he was a senior citizen with only a few years at most to live, and then he would face the Judgment. He could either face his Maker with a clear conscience, knowing he had done everything in his reasonable power to help the pastor succeed, or he could continue his current behavior and face an uncertain judgment.

The pastor closed his comments with a question: "Which path will you choose?" There was a long pause. The confronted bully left the office and stopped in the church lobby for a drink of water. He lingered long at the fountain. The pastor followed him to the water fountain awaiting an answer to his question.

The penitent church boss slowly raised his head, swept the pastor up in his arms in a massive bear hug, and said, "Pastor, you can count on me." From that moment, the former church boss was a changed man who worked in close harmony with the pastor.

Confrontation is a risky business, but sometimes it pays dividends. Usually, however, time and much patience is needed to win the love and respect of those who oppose our ministry vision for the church. The long-term pastorate provides this opportunity.

The apostle Paul, in some of his final words of advice to the young pastor Timothy, said:

> And the servant of the Lord must not strive; but be gentle unto all men, apt to teach, patient, in meekness instructing those that oppose themselves; if God peradventure will give them repentance to the acknowledging of the truth; and that they may recover themselves out of the snare of the devil, who are taken captive by him at his will (2 Timothy 2:24-26).

Here Paul was not speaking of opposition from outside the church; he was speaking to insiders. The young pastor was being harassed by older members of the congregation who were taking advantage of his tender age. Instead of being combative, Paul advised Timothy to be gentle and patient, meekly instructing those who opposed him.

"Who knows?" said Paul. They might see the error of their ways and repent. This would release them from the snare or entrapment of the devil who held them captive. It appears that local church bosses may be in the clutches of the devil without even realizing it.

Recapping the Chapter

There will come a time in every minister's life when he must decide to either stand and fight or leave his current post for a new challenge in the ministry. It is a time for deep soul-searching and seeking God earnestly in prayer for His divine will.

Some questions to consider include:

- Will staying be detrimental to the health and well-being of my family?

- Will staying enhance the growth and spiritual health of the congregation?

In short, will staying make a positive difference in the congregation you serve?

In the Old Testament, relocation was as simple as following the cloud of the presence of God. From the Day of Pentecost until modern times, the Spirit has become our guide. Stay sensitive to Him.

The current trend is toward the long-term pastorate. There are many advantages for the pastor and his family in ministering in one community for an extended period of time.

If you leave prematurely, the church boss wins the power struggle by default. If you stay, there is the possibility you may win the love and respect of the church boss.

And, oh yes, wherever you go, you will encounter a local church boss. They are everywhere.

14

Joy Comes in the Morning

Regardless of the tearing of the soul that the pastor and his family experience in doing battle with "the accuser of the brethren," there is joy and victory on the other side of the battle. This chapter offers more than a ray of hope that life will be good again. It is not only possible to survive combat with the local church boss, but it is also possible to actually thrive as a result of the conflict.

Jesus taught His disciples to have inner peace and joy even when they were being reviled and falsely accused. The psalmist said the Lord would prepare a banquet for him in the very presence of his enemies (Psalm 23:5). So it is possible to have joy in the midst of a conflict between the local church boss and the power structure of the church.

After Joshua and the armies of Israel had subdued their enemies, the Lord gave them a time of rest. This happened again generations later when David had defeated his enemies. A period of rest followed that lasted through Solomon's reign. God will give the pastor and his family periods of rest as well.

Peter and John rejoiced after their backs were lashed in the Temple for preaching about Jesus. They left the Temple rejoicing because they had been counted worthy to suffer for His name.

Paul and Silas sang praises to God from a damp, dark, rodent and lice-infested inner prison. Their backs were cut to ribbons by a guard wielding a cat-o'-nine-tails. And yet, they rejoiced at the midnight hour and sang praises to God. I don't understand this; but the love and grace of God can bring a song in the night. David said, "For his anger endureth but a moment; in his favour is life: weeping may endure for a night, but joy cometh in the morning" (Psalm 30:5).

If you and your family have been tried in the fire by doing battle with a local church boss, there will come a time when your body and spirit will need a period of rest and spiritual renewal. God loves you and knows what you need. He has a thousand ways to give you peace and rest. We will suggest only a few here.

The Short-Term Retreat

In a previous chapter, a working retreat for the pastor and staff was discussed. This is a mixture of productive work and therapeutic play. However, the idea here is not a working retreat but a time of relaxation and change of pace far from office phones and pastoral responsibilities—perhaps a cruise or a vacation in the mountains.

At one particularly busy time, Jesus said to His disciples, "Come ye yourselves apart into a desert place, and rest a while" (Mark 6:31). On this occasion the people were placing such demands on Jesus and His disciples they could not even find time to eat a meal together.

Much has been said about Jesus' use of the phrase "come ye . . . apart . . . and rest" with emphasis on the word *apart*." The intent of the commentary is to make the point that if you do not come *apart* and rest periodically, you will eventually come *apart* mentally, emotionally and physically.

Jesus could have called on His inner divine strength to continue ministering in spite of the heavy demands on His time and energy, but His disciples did not have this inner resource and neither do we. Jesus called for brief retreats from time to time for two reasons. First, He wanted to be an example to His disciples and future generations of ministers. Second, the human side of Jesus needed the rest.

The Sabbatical

Retreats are good, but they are relatively short in duration. Sometimes a longer period is needed to heal the wounds of the soul and find fresh anointing for your ministry.

The sabbatical is a concept borrowed from the world of academia. Colleges and universities often build a sabbatical into their operating budgets. Under this plan, a full-time professor may take up to a year off with pay after teaching seven years. Some travel to exotic places. Some go back to school. Others just play golf or go fishing. In any case, the professor returns to his duties refreshed and renewed in body and spirit, and culturally enriched.

Some churches are taking a look at this concept. Few local churches have the financial resources to offer this fringe benefit, but with proper planning they could be able to afford it. For example, suppose that when a new senior pastor takes office, the governing board offers him a salary and benefit package that includes a sabbatical. One-seventh of his pay is set aside each pay period on a matching-funds basis (church and pastor each contributing half). If this money were to be placed in an interest-bearing trust fund for seven years, there would be more than enough to finance a sabbatical. Should the pastor leave before seven years are up, the funds could be used as severance pay on a pro rata basis.

Some pastors object to this plan because they fear that the church would suffer from their long absence or be relieved they are gone. Others feel their temporary replacement may be so well liked that the congregation may prefer to keep him. These fears, even if they may contain a grain of truth, are mostly unfounded and fall into the category of unwarranted paranoia. The pastor who can spend a whole year away from his congregation will probably return with such renewed energy and enthusiasm that the congregation will reap many benefits.

My purpose here is not to argue the case for or against the sabbatical—it is to present an option for physical, mental, emotional and spiritual renewal. The sabbatical is just one option among many.

Change of Ministerial Roles

If you and your family have been badly hurt in battle with a local church boss, a sabbatical may not provide enough healing and recovery time. You may need to consider changing ministerial roles completely or even leaving the ministry for a while.

For example, if counseling is one of your strong points and your ministerial training provided adequate preparation in this field, you might find a position with a Christian counseling organization. However, if counseling does not fit your personality type, avoid this option. The last thing an emotionally distraught pastor would want to do is listen to other peoples' problems.

Do you remember being taught that *joy* can be an acronym for **J**esus, **O**thers and **Y**ou? It's true. As a dedicated Christian you have put Jesus first in your life. As a pastor, you have lived your life for others. Now it is time to complete your joy by adding the last element, "you." The psalmist said, "Restore unto me the joy of thy salvation" (Psalm 51:12). You need your joy back.

Forgiveness Brings Healing and Joy

Those who plan and promote fast-food franchise restaurants say the secret of success can be summed up in three words—location, location, location. The return of your inner peace and joy is also threefold—forgiveness, forgiveness, forgiveness.

Your wounded and bruised spirit cannot begin the healing process until you can forgive those who bruised and wounded you. Forgiveness is cathartic. It is like oil and wine being poured on the heads of the sheep by the caring shepherds (see Psalm 23:5).

Several months ago, one family in our local church suffered the tragic loss of a daughter in a brutal murder that is still unresolved. The mother often comes to me with tears in her eyes and malice in her heart toward those who murdered her child. Who could blame her? Our children are our most precious heritage. And yet, on several occasions I have advised her that healing cannot take place until she can find forgiveness in her heart. Admittedly, this is easier to say than to do. Yet, God himself had to forgive those who murdered His Son because Jesus asked Him to do so.

Whom do you need to forgive? For starters, how about forgiving your friends for not sticking by you when you needed them the most—Paul had to do that. Forgive your enemies, including the local church boss, because the Lord Jesus commands you to forgive. Forgive yourself for any real or perceived failure in your ministry. Forgive your ecclesiastical leader for assigning you to a questionable situation in the first place, and then being less than supportive when trouble erupted. Even forgive God for not rescuing you before you were put through the fiery trials that help to mold you into the image of His own dear Son.

I call this type of forgiveness the "stick" rule. Forgive those who did not *stick* by you, those who *stick* it to you, and yourself for not *sticking* it out in a bad situation. This might be called "The Golden Rule of Forgiveness."

Letters and Phone Calls

Hate mail (usually unsigned) and late-night harassing phone calls are commonly reported by the occupants of the parsonage. These acts, designed to disturb your rest and peace of mind, are often perpetrated directly by local church bosses or in proxy by weaker-minded folk over whom they wield a measure of influence.

How should a pastor react to these people? First, rejoice because these harassers definitely fall into the category of those who "say all manner of evil against you falsely, for [Christ's] sake" (Matthew 5:11). Then forgive them, for truly "they know not what they do" (Luke 23:34).

If we look for a Biblical precedent, the letter Sennacherib sent to King Hezekiah would fit the profile except the heathen king arrogantly signed the letter. King Hezekiah's reaction was to take the letter to the Temple, spread it out on the altar before the Lord, and pray a simple but effective prayer over it. The result was that God dispatched an angel who went through the camp of the Assyrians and executed 185,000 of them in one night (see 2 Kings 19:14-35).

One pastor reported that he first read a piece of unsigned hate mail to the congregation so they would be aware that someone with a poison pen was among them. Then after he and his wife had prayer over the letter, they burned it on the parking lot of the church as an act of sending it to God. The pressure was too much. The suspected letter writer moved the next week.

Harassing phone calls have been somewhat reduced since the introduction of Caller ID. However, if you continue to receive these calls, the matter should be turned over to the phone company for investigation and prosecution. Harassing or obscene phone calls are against the law.

Recapping the Chapter

Following periods of doing spiritual warfare with the local church boss, God will give His faithful ministers periods of rest and restoration. It is even possible to have inner peace and joy in the midst of conflict.

A few ways the pastor and his family may experience seasons of renewal and restoration include the short retreat or vacation, the one-year sabbatical, and the changing or exchanging of ministerial roles.

True healing and restoration of joy cannot begin to take place until the pastor forgives those who have wounded him—including the forgiving of the local church boss.

Harassing phone calls and anonymous hate mail should be handled in a spirit of love and forgiveness. However, when laws have been violated, the matter should be turned over to the proper authorities for investigation and prosecution. In the end, God will deal justly with those who harass or abuse His anointed leaders.

Endnotes

Introduction

[1] John C. Maxwell, *Developing the Leader Within You* (Nashville: Thomas Nelson, 1993).

Chapter 1

[1] The definition of the phrase terroronicus pastors (the terror of pastors) cannot be located in any Latin to English dictionary. The author coined the phrase to fit the description and perception of the local church boss.

[2] John Foxe, Foxe's Book of Martyrs, ed.W. Grinton Berry (Grand Rapids, Michigan: Baker Book House Publishers, 1998).

Chapter 2

[1] Walt Kelly, "Pogo." Syndicated Cartoon. (Earth Day, 1971).

Chapter 4

[1] *Sleeping With The Enemy* (Produced and Directed by Twentieth Century Fox) 1990.

[2] Tim Kimmel, *How To Deal With Powerful Personalities* (Colorado Springs, Colorado: Focus On The Family, 1994) 13.

[3] Kimmel, 106.

[4] Kimmel, 83.

[5] Kimmel, 108.

Chapter 5
[1] Oliver McMahan, *Becoming A Shepherd* (Cleveland, TN: Pathway Press, 1994), 39.

Chapter 6
[1] Laurence J. Peter and Raymond Hull, *The Peter Principle* (New York: William Morrow, 1969).
[2] John Humble, *Management By Objectives* (Toronto, Canada: Coles, 1980).
[3] Eric E. Anschutz, *TQM America* (Bradenton, Florida: McGuinn & McGuire, 1995).
[4] Gerald L. Gutek, *Cultural Foundations of Education* (New York: MacMillan, 1991) 345-365.
[5] Kenneth Estell, ed., *African-American Almanac* (Detroit: Gale) 41.
[6] Robert G. Owens, *Organizational Behavior in Schools* (Englewood Cliffs, NJ: Prentice-Hall, 1970) 4.
[7] Ibid., 5-6.
[8] Ibid., 9-10.
[9] John Neisbitt and Patricia Aburdene, *Megatrends 2000* (New York: Avon , 1990) xiii.

Chapter 8
[1] Brooks Jackson, *Jimmy Carters' Killer Rabbit* (Associate Press), 1979.
[2] *Fiddler on the Roof,* Broadway Musical produced and directed by Norman Jewison, 1971.

Chapter 9
[1] *Webster's II New Riverside Dictionary* (New York: Berkley, 1986) 680.

² Ibid., 699.

³ At Home With the Arctic Wolf," *National Geographic*, vol. 171, no. 5 (Washington, DC: NGS, May 1987) 584- 592.

⁴ Robert Wallace and the Editors of Time-Life Books, *The Italian Campaign* (Alexandria, VA: Time-Life, 1978) 134, 135.
John Toland, *Battle: The Story of the Bulge* (New York: Random, 1959).
John Strawson, *The Battle for Berlin* (New York: Scribner's, 1974).

⁵ John Bartlett, *Familiar Quotations* 16ᵗʰ edition, (Boston: Little, 1992) 496.

⁶ Daniel E. Sutterland, *Fredericksburg & Chancellorsville: The Dare Mark Campaign* (Lincoln: U of Neb P, 1998).
Voices of the Civil War*Gettysburg by the Editors of Time-Life Books, (Alexandria, VA: Time-Life, 1995).

⁷ John Keegan, *Fields of Battle: The Wars for North America* (New York: Knopf, 1996) 167.

⁸ Max Hastings, *Overlord D-Day, June 6, 1944* (New York: Simon, 1984).

Chapter 10

¹ William Whiston, A. M. Trans. *The Works of Josephus* (Peabody, MA: Hendrickson, 1987) Chapter 1; Section 5.

² James Strong, *Strong's Exhaustive Concordance of the Bible* (Peabody, MA: Hendrickson Publishers, n.d.), angel (#G32).

Chapter 11

[1] Carl R. Hobbs, ed., *Mutual Expectations Covenant* (Unpublished Document).

Chapter 12

[1] *Strongs,* preeminence (G5383).
[2] *Strongs,* prating (#H8193).
[3] *Strongs*, prating (#G5396).

Chapter 13

[1] John Maxwell, *Developing the Leader Within You* (Nashville: Thomas Nelson, 1993) 17-20.